THE WINNER'S WAY

*A Transactional Analysis Guide for Living,
Working, and Learning*

THE WINNER'S WAY

A Transactional Analysis Guide for Living, Working, and Learning

Gisele Weisman
Georgia State University

Brooks/Cole Publishing Company
Monterey, California
A Division of Wadsworth, Inc.

Printed in the United States of America

10 9 8 7 6 5 4 3 2 1

Library of Congress Cataloging in Publication Data

Weisman, Gisele
    The winner's way.

    Includes index.
    1. Transactional analysis.   2. Self-perception.
3. Success.   I. Title.
RC489.T7W43   616.8'914   79-18925
ISBN 0-8185-0350-5

Acquisition Editor: *Claire Verduin*
Project Development Editor: *Ray Kingman*
Production Editor: *Sally Schuman*
Interior and Cover Design: *Ruth Scott*
Typesetting: *David R. Sullivan Company, Dallas, Texas*

Preface

The Winner's Way: A Transactional Analysis Guide for Living, Working, and Learning presents a Transactional Analysis model for clarifying and achieving personal, educational, and vocational goals. It is both an introduction to TA as a theory of personality and technique of psychotherapy and a guide to using TA concepts to increase self-awareness and effect personal and career change. Because of its two-fold nature—as an introduction to TA and a workbook for personal growth—the book can be used in a wide variety of courses, ranging from introductory psychology to personal development, life/career planning, and human relations.

Section I, entitled "Who Am I?", presents the basic concepts of Transactional Analysis, including the *Adult, Parent,* and *Child ego states,* the *ego-state portrait,* the *life position,* and the *life script,* and discusses how these concepts relate to our feelings, behaviors, and interactions with others. The section concludes with a Seven-Step Action Plan for setting and pursuing goals that involve personal change and invites the reader to write a contract with himself or herself for reaching a chosen goal. Each of the next two sections—"Where Am I Going?" and "How Do I Get There?"—follows the format presented in Section I. Again using the terms and concepts of TA as a model, the reader explores the process of setting and reaching work- and school-related goals. The last chapter in each of these sections shows how to apply the Seven-Step Action Plan to vocational and educational aims.

Each chapter of the book concludes with a section of exercises designed to serve two purposes: First, they help the reader explore and understand better the principles of Transactional Analysis. And second, they invite the reader to consider in more depth his or her own feelings, thoughts, and actions in order to enhance self-understanding and facilitate change. Some of the exercises involve group discussion or role playing; others involve only the individual reader. Some require action; others consist of thinking about important life issues. In doing the exercises, the reader has the opportunity to begin the process of change within the simple and effective framework of Transactional Analysis.

I would like to acknowledge and thank the many people who reviewed and commented on the manuscript in its various stages: Ronald D. Bingham, Brigham Young University; Charlotte L. Blee, Tallahassee Community College; Dennis Coon, Santa Barbara City College; William J. Jacobs, Lake City Community College; Richard T. Laird, Citrus College; Lynette Long, The Catholic University of America; Jean R. Marton, Los Angeles Harbor College; Robert Schwartz, Pasadena City College; Dru Spiro, Lincoln Land Community College; Velma Walker, Tarrant County Junior College; and Kathy West, Portland Community College. In addition, I want to express my gratitude to my friends and colleagues who read the manuscript in its developmental stages and offered valuable suggestions, many of which I have incorporated into the book: Joan Elifson, Georgia State University; John Kohler III, Clayton Junior College; Richard Rank, Georgia State University; Gene Minor, Colorado Mountain College; and Anthony Cocoran.

Gisele Weisman

Contents

vii

THE WINNER'S WAY

A Transactional Analysis Guide for Living,
Working, and Learning

Introduction

This book is written for people who either are about to encounter or have encountered a situation requiring that they adopt a new direction in life. People who graduate from high school, lose a job, terminate a marriage, or wish to make career or life-style changes are asking questions such as "What should I do now?" "How do I know that what I'm getting into is what's best for me?" "How do I find out what I really want to do?" and "How do I pick from the many alternatives the world has to offer me?" Because such questions often go unanswered or are only partially explored, people sometimes find themselves doing what others feel they should do or repeating what they've habitually done in the past. Breaking old habits and successfully making the transition to the "new you" require a solid understanding of "Who am I?" "Where am I going?" and "How do I get there?" Sections I, II, and III of this book deal with precisely these three questions.

The first section—"Who Am I?"—focuses on intrapersonal concerns, or concerns within the self. It not only is designed to help you become aware of what your ingrained coping strategies are, where they came from, and how they have shaped and molded your current way of doing things but also provides you with the opportunity to reevaluate those strategies and, if you like, adopt new coping skills. As you become more aware of who you are, you may find that you are satisfied with your current coping strategies, and you will therefore feel more confident and secure in continuing with what you're already doing. If, however, you find that you would benefit from making major or minor changes in how you cope, the concluding chapter in the first section of this book, which outlines and demonstrates the use of a change strategy—the Seven-Step Action Plan—will prove useful.

Section II—"Where Am I Going?"—focuses on making major life decisions, such as those pertaining to career, family, school, and life-style. Section III—"How Do I Get There?"—discusses traditional versus nontraditional attitudes toward goal attainment and examines the kinds of barriers people often use to block themselves from reaching

1

their goals. It also explores how to remove those barriers. Since "getting there," more often than not, involves choosing a career or adopting a more desirable way of earning a living and since most occupations require prior training, Section II will focus on vocational concerns and Section III on how to survive the training or school experience.

Although there are many "how to do it" books on the market that readers around the world have found useful and enriching, this book represents the first effort to apply Eric Berne's Transactional Analysis (TA) psychotherapeutic model collectively to personal, vocational, and educational issues. The TA approach was selected for this book simply because its down-to-earth, nontechnical, and easy-to-use concepts and language make it possible to deal with these three major life areas in a single volume. Methods for clarifying and attaining goals can be learned in a school quarter or semester. The ability to apply labels or use a new vocabulary doesn't constitute knowledge or understanding, however. It is the commitment to helping yourself interpersonally, vocationally, and educationally that can make these terms and concepts useful and valuable to you.

In 1964 Eric Berne brought TA to the attention of the general public in his popular book *Games People Play.* In 1969 Thomas Harris published *I'm OK— You're OK* and helped millions of people become more aware of their feelings—good and bad—toward themselves and others. TA has been recognized as a useful conceptual model for dealing with the diverse concerns of everyday life, and it has been applied to personal development, vocational settings, and school environments in a wide range of books: *Born to Love: TA in the Church* (James, 1973); *Dealing with the Public: TA for Employees and Their Supervisors* (Burke, 1976); *Games Alcoholics Play* (Steiner, 1971); *TA for Moms and Dads* (James, 1974); *What Do You Say After You Say "Hello"?* (Berne, 1972); and *Ten Ways to Begin the School Year With TA: A Handbook of TA Lesson Plans for Teachers* (D'Angelo, 1974).

At this point, a quick overview of TA terms and concepts will help you establish a conceptual framework for what follows.

Ego States

According to TA people's behaviors can be categorized into three distinct and very different states of being. These very real and observable states of being are the *Parent ego state,* the *Child ego state,* and the *Adult ego state.** People who are in the Parent ego state behave pretty much like typical authority figures—parents, bosses, and teachers, who dictate what we should or shouldn't do. TA recognizes both OK Parent messages, which comfort and nurture, and not-OK Parent messages, which are debilitating and harmful. OK Parent messages put reasonable controls or limits on behavior—"Look both ways before crossing the street"—and comfort—"That's all right, you can work it out." Not-OK Parent messages are unreasonable statements such as "You're too stupid to do anything right."

The Child ego state is the emotional or "feeling" part of the self. The Child can be *Natural* or totally free to express spontaneously whatever comes to mind. Whether or not the behavior is appropriate is irrelevant to the Natural Child. The Child can also be *Adaptive,* or eager to please and conforming to social commandments or *injunctions* that are typically dictated by the Parent ego state. Finally, the Child can be *Creative.* This Creative Child is often referred to as the "Little Professor" because it knows how to get what it wants, to get out of uncomfortable situations or into desirable situations.

The Adult ego state is the self's rational computer; it processes information and makes decisions. The Adult is only as good as the data it has to work with: if you're operating from accurate data, then you're *uncontaminated,* but, if you're operating on limited or inaccurate data, then you're *contaminated* and vulnerable to ineffective or inappropriate decisions. The uncontaminated well-functioning Adult knows how to screen and process the data received from the Child ego state and the Parent ego state and maintains a balance between these two very different and often opposing forces. (For a graphic picture of the ego states see Figure 1-1.)

Life Positions

Your ego-state composition, or how your ego states function as a total unit, determines your *life position* or "basic attitude in life." According to TA there are four basic life positions:

I'm OK, You're OK
I'm not-OK, You're OK

---

*When the terms *Parent, Child,* and *Adult* are capitalized in this book, they refer to these TA ego states.

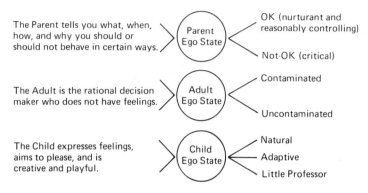

Figure 1-1. Ego states.

I'm OK, You're not-OK
I'm not-OK, You're not-OK

TA theory says that your life position, or attitude toward yourself and others, was determined in childhood. A child, in response to his or her environment, makes a pre-mature decision about how to live in order to survive. Typically this pre-mature life position implies numerous injunctions or commandments that the child has not thought through but has chosen to live by. These injunctions may lose their appropriateness as the child matures and becomes aware of how he or she is interacting with others, but, unless they are challenged or questioned, they will continue to govern his or her life.

Life Script

Your ego-state composition is also revealed in your *life script*, which was also developed in childhood. According to TA, your life script is a conclusion you reached about how you have to behave in order to survive in this world. Since behavior patterns are set in childhood, the tendency is to repeat these same patterns throughout life.

Time Structuring

TA holds that, by *structuring time* through *withdrawals, rituals, pastimes, activities*, and/or *games*, we protect ourselves from "real" or *intimate* contact with the self and/or others. This book's point of view is that understanding and knowing how to utilize withdrawals, rituals, pastimes, activities, and games can help us bridge communication gaps and increase intimacy.

Strokes

In addition to the way we structure time, we also utilize *strokes* to communicate with each other. *Positive strokes* say "I like you," and *negative strokes* say "I don't like you." *Conditional strokes* say "I will like you *if* and *only if* you do such and such" and *unconditional strokes* say "I am willing to accept you for who you are and negotiate our differences."

Transactions

A *transaction* consists of a verbal or nonverbal exchange between two or more people. Transactions also occur within you among your own Parent, Adult, and Child. Through analyzing units of transaction we can increase our understanding of what is communicated inter- and intrapersonally. The basic goal of this book is to gain an in-depth understanding of the questions: "How are my *ego states* (values, reasoning power, and feelings) reflected in my *life position* (attitude) and my *life script* (behavior patterns), and how do I *structure time* and *stroke* in order to communicate, or *transact,* my *position* and *script* to others?"

The best approach to learning about yourself is a positive attitude that allows you to take an honest and open look at who you are. As a result of reading this book you may find that you really like who you are, where you're going, and how you've decided to get there. You may also discover the opposite to be true, or you may be somewhere in between. Before you undertake your own action plan, check yourself out and confirm for yourself that you are, in fact, doing what's best for you. So try to embark on this book with the following attitude: "I want to get a clear picture of who I am; I want to make sure that where I'm going is a good place for me to be; and I would like to reach my goal with a minimum of strife and detour."

Section I

WHO AM I?

Our lives consist of situations involving love, intimacy, beliefs, attitudes, sexuality, parenthood, death, work, and play. We can't escape coming face-to-face with these human experiences, but we can do something about how we respond to them. In this section of the book, we will not deal with these situations specifically but, rather, will focus on coping strategies that pertain to any and every situation. It will enable you to take a good look at who you are and how you currently cope or avoid coping and at whether you would like to improve, change, or add to your coping skills. The goal is to help you become aware of who is actually making your decisions, how you feel inside, how you process information, and how your attitude toward yourself and others influences how you cope.

Your behavior patterns and feelings determine the outcome of everything that you undertake or encounter. It's therefore important that you know what you're doing, how you're feeling, how what you're doing affects you and others, and whether you would like to enhance, alter, or change your behavior. We often wish for better coping skills, but we either don't know how or won't make the effort to get what we want. Knowing what you want won't make it automatically happen, but, as you read this first section, you will become familiar with what you want. Whether you will do something about it is up to you, and the seven-step action plan that concludes this first section will show you how to systematically change what you want to change.

Identifying your PARENT

How much control do you have over your own life? How many of the decisions you make are really your own? Are you aware of the disciplining rules and regulations you allow to influence you daily? Do you know where these rules and regulations came from in the first place? By taking a good look at what TA calls the *Parent ego state* you will be able to answer these questions.

The Parent ego state is the part of you that stores messages like this:

"You should speak only when you're spoken to."
"You shouldn't let others know how you feel."
"You ought to have more sense."
"You shouldn't stay out late."
"You shouldn't spend your time or money foolishly."
"Stop smoking."
"Start jogging, it's good for you."

We all carry messages like these with us wherever we go, and we allow them to influence much of what we do. It isn't very often, however, that we pause to question where these messages came from in the first place. They came from those people who said "I told you so." "You should have listened to me." "You made your bed, now lie in it." "Can't you do anything right?" They also came from those who said "I love you." "We'll make it all better." "I am so proud of you." "You make me happy." They came from those people who hugged, kissed, spanked, and smiled and frowned at you. They came from parents, relatives, older brothers and sisters, and other important people in your life. They also came from friends and perhaps even from television, movies, and characters in books.

As children, everyone eagerly models those they value, right or wrong, good or bad. This doesn't mean that they necessarily like (or dislike) their models. Rather, they idolize those who are capable of satisfying their wants and needs. Thus, you had no choice as to which Parent messages you adopted, and you helplessly and naively allowed these Parent messages to shape your personality and life-style. You were born to and associated with people who had experienced life and who had learned the skills they needed in order to survive in the world. They, in turn, set out as best they knew to teach you those skills. They interpreted and represented society through their own understanding of right and wrong and gave you a set of injunctions, or commandments, to live by.

While growing up you heard certain Parent messages over and over again; you adapted yourself to them, internalized them, and made them your own. The message "You always say the wrong thing" becomes "I always say the wrong thing." "You better look both ways before crossing the street" becomes "I better look both ways before crossing the street." "You're stupid" becomes "I'm stupid." You may ask "What exactly made me swallow these messages whole without looking first to see whether or not they suited me personally?" As a child you didn't have the reasoning power to sift and sort through these messages, nor did you have the life experience to allow you to evaluate grown-ups' standards. As a consequence it was easier to observe and model those who were bigger and, seemingly, wiser than you. Your dependency and fear of losing their love, combined with their disciplinary tactics, left you virtually no choice but to conform.

As we grow older, we become more and more accustomed to the rules and regulations we were raised with, and soon we claim them as our very own. As time passes we forget that those coping strategies were, in fact, adopted from others; we begin to think "This is me!" Once this happens we no longer have a need for others to tell us what, when, and how to do things, because our private collection of Parent messages has become our Parent ego state that we play, rewind, and replay as needed.

Perhaps it's time that you examine the commandments you live by and determine whether or not they are appropriate to your desired way of living. Some of the messages you adopted are vital to your general well-being, but others are not. After you take the time to examine them, place yourself in the position to decide which ones are best suited to you, eliminate the ones that are inappropriate, and build on and improve the ones that are already working for you. This is a private and very personal matter, because what may be considered "generally" appropriate may not be right for you. For example, a traditional Parent message is to "clean your plate." If you're skinny, you may want to hold on to that message, but, if you are overweight, then that one may be inappropriate for you.

Examining the rules and regulations you have blindly claimed as your own is important for another reason, too. These are also the messages you give to others. Our habit is to adopt an unconscious pattern that goes something like this:

"What they wanted from me, I now want for myself and from others."
"What they did to me, I will now do to myself and to others."
"The way they controlled me, I will now control myself and others."
"They manipulated me, and now I am using the same tactics to manipulate myself and others."

The following story illustrates how Parent messages are learned at a very young age and are passed from generation to generation.

Little 3-year-old Lucy was playing with her doll. She cuddled it, dressed it, changed its diapers, and fed it. Suddenly she slapped the doll's hand and screamed at it "I told you not to play with your food. Look at you. You are a mess. Mommy only loves clean little girls. If you don't stop throwing food around, Mommy will spank you. You bad girl!" Lucy's mother, shocked by her child's behavior, rushed to the scene and wanted to know what Lucy was doing. Lucy looked up, smiled, and said "I'm teaching my baby to behave just like you teach me, Mommy."

Later Lucy was playing with Bobby, her little 4-year-old brother. As they were riding their tricycles, Bobby lost control, fell off, and badly skinned himself. Lucy ran to him and said "Bobby, don't move, you'll be alright. I'll be right back with Mommy."

By age 3, Lucy had already learned how to raise her own children, and her children will probably learn those same child-rearing techniques to pass on to their children. Unless someone along the line stops to ask whether these Parent messages are relevant, healthy, or appropriate, the messages will be incorporated as they are. There are, without a doubt, Parent messages that are not only helpful but actually vital to our survival. But there are others that may be harmful, destructive, or irrelevant and need to be reexamined and perhaps altered or discarded. It is often difficult to give yourself permission to change self-imposed standards, because to break your own rules is to upset your own value system. It is often not only difficult but also threatening to give up something that has worked, for others and for you, but that may no longer be relevant or appropriate for you. Unless you find a new set of rules that work for you or adjust the old set, you'll hang on to your traditional way of coping.

Although our Parent messages do serve as coping strategies for most of the situations we encounter, there seems to be a lack of Parent messages for the many predicaments and first-time experiences that are a part of modern-day living. Because the world is changing more rapidly today than ever before, it's often difficult to understand what's happening around us. Some situations of life are so very new and different that there are no traditional Parent messages for them, and we are forced to quickly establish Parent messages that will keep us safe.

Traditionally, life as a single person was regarded as, at best, a temporary situation, experienced by people who waited anxiously to get married. Today more and more people are choosing to be single. Old stereotypes and stigmas of the single life may be disappearing; that is, singles may no longer be viewed as life's lonely losers. But, in adopting this life-style, single people find themselves in an atypical situation for which there are no traditional Parent messages. For instance, they may ask "How do I behave in singles' bars?" "How do I meet people?" "What do I do when I get lonely?" "Should I go out at night by myself?"

Because many single people simply don't know what to do when they are confronted with such first-time situations, they may quickly copy what their friends are doing. Trying out different behaviors until you find what fits you and adopting that as a part of your Parent ego state is a way of filling in the coping-skill gaps. You are, however, the sum total of your past life experiences. You may need to live with your newly adopted values for a while in order to find out whether they fit with the total sum of who you are. If you were raised with "Don't take candy from strangers," you may find it difficult to accept a drink from a total stranger in a singles' bar. You may or may not be able to overcome this fear, and that depends to some degree on how you want to integrate your present and future with the traditional you.

Although we're living in changing times, it's impractical to forget that those people who taught us our values still feel responsible for shaping our lives and therefore continue to remind us of how we should and shouldn't think, feel, and behave. We're often confronted with familiar messages of the "do as I do" or "do as I say, not as I do" types. These may be in direct conflict with the modern coping strategies we are trying out. The "do as I do" type may include:

> "I went to college, and, therefore, you will go to college."
> "I made it without an education, so I don't see why you need one."
> "I got married when I was young; I don't see why you're stalling."

The "do as I say, not as I do" type may include:

> "I got pregnant and had to get married; now don't you go fooling around."
> "If only I had had the opportunity to go to college, I could have been somebody."
> "Be honest and polite, and don't you let me catch you doing what I just did."

Now that we have acquainted ourselves with the concept of Parent messages that constitute our Parent ego state, let's take a look at the different kinds of Parent messages. TA identifies two distinct and different types of Parents: the *Nurturing* Parent and the *Controlling* Parent. The Nurturing Parent is capable of giving comfort and support. To use the Nurturing Parent wisely is to know how to be good to yourself. Do you have a favorite person you can go to, no matter how unbearable things get, and know that that person will make you feel better, no matter who's at fault? If you can do for yourself what that person does for you, then you know what it means to have a Nurturing Parent within. Your Nurturing Parent can help you work yourself out of feelings of hurt, failure, or depression. It can put its arms around you and say "I can make things work out" or "Anyone can make a mistake." You can learn how to make yourself feel like you're hugging yourself from the inside out and become your own best friend.

The Controlling Parent can be OK Critical or not-OK Critical. The OK Critical Parent is mindful of what's necessary to keep you safe. It keeps you in line with helpful shoulds and shouldn'ts such as "Bundle up, it's cold outside," "Don't eat too fast, you'll get indigestion," "Don't forget to say please and thank you." This Parent reminds you of pleasant, and not-so-pleasant, social duties and niceties. It likes you to be punctual and gets annoyed when you're inconsiderate or unkind to others. Whenever you impose *reasonable* demands on yourself, you are allowing your OK Critical Parent to be your friend. Superstitions can be OK critical messages as long as they are used in fun rather than fear. Messages like "Don't walk under ladders" and "Turn back if a black cat crosses your path" have been handed down from generation to generation and are indicative of how Parent messages survive for centuries after they are no longer useful.

The not-OK Critical Parent imposes *unreasonable* demands on you. This parent can make life unbearable because it loves to make you feel inferior, incompetent, stupid, untrustworthy, clumsy, or ugly. Whenever you experience such negative feelings, your not-OK Parent is closing in on you, and you become your own worst enemy. An easy way to detect that harmful Parent is to listen to it. It likes to speak in absolutes like "always," "never," "forever," and "definitely." Statements such as "You *always* say the wrong thing," "You *never* do anything right," "You are *forever* taking others for granted," and "You are *definitely* boring" come from this Parent. This Parent also loves to exaggerate and uses words like "ugliest," "worst," "stupid," and "incompetent": "That's the *ugliest* painting you've painted yet," "That's the *worst* decision you could have made," "You are really *stupid,*" "You are *incompetent.*"

Parent messages are communicated verbally and nonverbally. Demands, commands, sarcastic remarks, gentle hints, certain understood facial expressions or postures, or even silence can communicate what, when, and how you should or should not behave. It's not difficult to remember that look, that understood moment of silence, or that "kind" remark that left no doubt as to what was expected of you and may have even left you feeling severely reprimanded.

How much control do you have over your own life? Who makes your decisions for you? You are now acquainted with the concept of Parent messages and are consequently in a better position to look at who you are. Perhaps it's time to ask yourself: "Am I happy? Am I getting what I want out of life? What am I going to do about it?" As a child you may have been helpless against the injunctions that were imposed on you. You weren't in a position to choose. What's stopping you now?

Keep in mind that you are your past and you are becoming your future. The idea is not to start "cleaning house" and throwing out Parent messages but, rather, to select the best from the old, integrate that with the present, try it all out, experience the results of your decisions, and collect what works for you. You will repeat this process for the rest of your life. If you want to alter or replace a Parent message, then the seven-step action plan at the end of this section will help you do that.

The exercises that follow are designed to help you get in touch with how you are allowing your Parent messages to regulate your life. As you check out your current value system, try to tune in to what you like and dislike about yourself and how you would like to change that. As a result of these exercises you may find that you either have or have not received the kind of commandments or injunctions that are appropriate to your daily living. You may learn that you may or may not be giving yourself and others enough Nurturing Parent messages. You may also discover that you have been unreasonably critical and demanding of yourself and others. You owe it to yourself to become aware of who you are and who you would like to be.

Exercises

Individual Activity: The Nurturing Parent

Are you your own best friend? Do you think that you can become your own best friend or at least a good friend to yourself? Let's explain your Nurturing Parent by first looking at the nurturing people in your past, then at those in your present, and finally at your own nurturing qualities. Remember that nurturing people in your life may include relatives, friends, TV and movie personalities, fictional and nonfictional personalities in novels and textbooks, and recording artists.

Let's first focus on your past. Ask yourself the following questions and answer them thoughtfully. Write down your answers:

1. Whom did I enjoy spending time with?
2. Whom did I turn to when I was in trouble?
3. Whom did I consider to be wise and insightful?
4. Who said the kinds of things that were comforting and soothing?
5. Who made me feel protected?
6. Which stories made me feel warm and secure?
7. Which songs gave me something comforting to hold on to?

Now focus on what the Nurturing Parent messages actually were.

1. What did "they" do that was kind?
2. What did "they" do that was helpful?
3. What did "they" do that made you feel safe and protected?
4. What were the messages that pleasantly lingered in your mind?
5. How did "they" go about giving comfort and advice?
6. How did "they" behave physically? That is, did they hug, kiss, and cuddle?
7. How did "they" dress?
8. What were "their" likes and dislikes?

Now focus on your current sources of nurturing.

1. Who and what currently provides you with the nurturing you need and want?
2. Do you provide yourself as well as others with this nurturing?
3. How have you recently nurtured others?
4. How have you recently nurtured yourself?
5. Whose nurturing qualities have you copied?
6. What are the nurturing qualities of others in your past and present? (Include behaviors, appearances, and verbal communications.)

Class Activity: The OK Critical Parent

To become aware of your OK Critical Parent is to check out the helpful rules and regulations you live by. Discussing the following items in class will give each class member the opportunity to identify and clarify the various values different people accept and live by.

1. As a group, make a list of helpful rules and regulations you live by or feel you should live by.
2. Discuss where these rules and regulations came from.
3. Remember that every person lives by different rules and regulations. Discuss what is and is not helpful to you and why it is or isn't relevant to your life-style.
4. Discuss the OK Critical Parent messages you have imposed on others and why you expect others to respect them.

Individual Activity: The OK Critical Parent

Think about the following questions:

1. What are some rules and regulations that you respect but that are no longer relevant to you?
2. What is it about them that no longer fits your life-style?
3. Which ones are you willing to keep and why?
4. Which ones would you like to alter?
5. Which ones are you willing to discard and why?
6. What are you imposing on others that you feel is fair?
7. What are you imposing on others that you would like to reconsider?
8. What are you imposing on others that you should reconsider although you really don't want to?

Individual Activity: The Not-OK Critical Parent

It may be painful for you to identify who made and is making you feel unloved, insignificant, stupid, clumsy, worthless, or irresponsible. It may be even more painful to discover how you are hurting yourself. But in coming to grips with what is causing you pain you will understand what you would like to do about it. The following questions will help you clarify not only where your not-OK Critical Parent messages come from but also how you may be perpetuating them.

1. Make a list of the people you knew as a child who made you feel unloved, insignificant, clumsy, worthless, irresponsible, and so on.
2. What did they say?
3. What did they do?
4. How did they behave?
5. What options did they have?
6. How did they dress?
7. What did you do to protect yourself when these not-OK Critical Parent messages were directed toward you?
8. What do you currently do to protect yourself?
9. What would you like to change?

Now take an honest look at yourself.

1. What do you do to yourself that resembles what "they" did to you?
2. What do you say to yourself that resembles what "they" said about you?
3. What would you like to change or get rid of?
4. What do you do to others that resembles what "they" did to you?
5. What do you say to others that resembles what "they" said to you?
6. What would you like to change or get rid of?

Small-Group Activity: The Not-OK Critical Parent

Share with one another some of the painful experiences in your life (talk about those you don't mind sharing). Discuss what made them so painful. Discuss how telling about the situation makes you feel. Do you feel anger, hate, helplessness? Do you feel sorry for yourself? How long have these feelings been hanging on? Help one another think of OK ways to deal with these feelings.

Now share with one another some things you have done to others that you wish you hadn't done (talk only about those you don't mind sharing). Discuss how they resemble the behavior of those people who hurt you. Discuss what you would do if you could go back and change things. Critique each other's solutions and discuss how they would make you feel if you were the receiving party.

Class Activity: The Parent Ego State

Consider the following situations and solve them first as a Nurturing Parent, then as an OK Critical Parent, and finally as a not-OK Critical Parent. Don't limit yourself just to what you would say. Include what you would do, how you would act, and what you would wear. In addition to the following situations, add your own.

1. Your spouse has just informed you that your mother-in-law, whom you've never liked and can't get along with, will be arriving the next day and plans to stay for a week.
2. Your best friend broke a date with you because someone she

or he would rather go out with that night just became available.

3. Your parents invite you to Sunday dinner, and you have already made other plans.
4. Your roommate insists on playing records every time you get ready to study.
5. Your child is calling for someone to "come and look." Since you are studying for an exam, you wait a minute to see if your spouse will tend to it. Nothing happens. The child calls again.
6. The person you have been dating makes you feel like you always come last, and you're tired of not coming first.
7. An irresponsible friend has just lost his or her job and is blaming everyone but himself or herself.
8. Bob has just broken up with Jane, and she has come to you in tears. She feels like she is at fault and desperately wants him back.
9. A friend has just lost $50, which you know was hard-earned money, and has come to tell you about it. Your friend feels not only foolish and irresponsible but also self pitying. This friend needs that money and doesn't know what to do.
10. You've just observed a 6-year-old fall off her skateboard. The child is hurt and crying.

Individual Activity: The Parent Ego State

Getting in touch with when and how you and others use the three different Parents will help you decide whether or not you would like to change how your Parent operates. For three or four days keep track of the circumstances under which you and those you encounter utilize the Nurturing, OK Critical, and not-OK Critical Parents.

Class Activity: The Parent Ego State

Creating new Parent messages may be both fun and interesting. Identify first-time experiences you or your friends have recently encountered. Talk about how you or your friends coped with them. As a group, suggest additional ways of dealing with these situations. The following are the kinds of situations you may want to deal with.

1. "I have never shared in household responsibilities, and now my spouse expects me to do half of everything. I don't know how to cook or wash clothes. I don't even know whether I want to learn."
2. "I'm single and am raising two kids. How do I go about meeting people I can go out with, and how do I explain my dating to the children?"
3. "I knew how to behave on a date when I was in my teens. But I've been married for fifteen years, I am recently divorced, and I don't know how to behave on a date."
4. "I'm gay. My problem is, how do I go about telling my folks?"

"How do I feel inside?" 2

Identifying your CHILD

Whenever you experience a feeling such as joy, anger, pain or comfort, you're in your *Child ego state*. Your Child reacts to your Parent messages, and your Parent does its very best to control your feelings, or that Child within you. Whenever you are experiencing internal conflict, you may want to check out what's going on inside your head. You may find that your conflict is due to a power struggle between your Parent and your Child. A typical dialogue between these two ego states may sound something like this:

Parent: "You shouldn't order another drink."
Child: (Belches.)
Parent: "Mind your manners."
Child: "Well, OK, you're right, I'll finish this drink and go home."
Parent: "That's more like it, you know what it's like to wake up with a hang-over."
Child: "Yes, I know, you're absolutely right." (Continues to order several more drinks.)

TA identifies three very different Children within us. An example of each Child has been given in the above dialogue between Parent and Child. The first response to the Parent, the belch, is from the Natural Child. The "good" Child that listened to the Parent is the Adaptive Child, and the Child that appeared to conform but continued drinking is the Little Professor. Let's take a closer look at how each of these Children functions.

21

Can you remember how, as a child, you used to play, explore, run, hug, kiss, taste, and cry? Are you able to recall the sense of freedom that enabled you to feel impulsively and spontaneously with every inch of your being and to express those feelings fully and completely? You had no self-control or discipline whatsoever, no bathroom habits, no manners of any kind, no shoulds or shouldn'ts. You simply behaved *naturally,* without inhibitions. You were "untrained," the natural you, your Natural Child. Of course, some natural behaviors like belching, picking your nose, or throwing temper tantrums at any time and any place are undesirable, and we appreciate the Parent messages that teach us what is and isn't acceptable socially. Sometimes, however, we allow Parent messages to mold and shape that Natural Child out of existence. To lose that Natural Child is to lose the ability to be inventive, adventurous, curious, sentimental, sensuous, fun-loving, angry, sad, hurt, happy, rebellious, and stubborn. In short, it's to lose the ability to respond according to the way we really feel inside.

To pay attention to your Natural Child is to check out gut-level feelings about the decisions you make. If you really listen to yourself, your Natural Child won't lie to you. You may not be telling yourself what you want to hear, but you won't be dishonest with yourself. Too frequently, however, the tendency is to ignore or suppress the Natural Child. How many times have you told yourself not to feel the way you feel? How many times have you denied yourself the opportunity to really get close to your feelings of depression, anger, joy, love, and hate?

Your Natural Child can be the most rewarding and enjoyable or the most destructive and embarrassing part of your personality. To let it come out fully is to let yourself enjoy the freedom you enjoyed as a child. As an adult, you will want to regulate when to lose control and when to recapture your Natural Child's capacity to express itself honestly and openly.

We often deny feelings because we don't really know how to cope with them. Our Parent messages often tell us not to "feel" or, if we do feel, not to show those feelings. If our goal is to deny the existence of our feelings, then we've been busy developing strategies for covering them up rather than coping with them. If we check out our Parent messages, we'll find that most messages pertaining to coping with spontaneous self-expression are condescending and condemning. The Natural Child, is, however, becoming a more acceptable part of social interaction. Parent messages are changing to include strategies that tell us how to accept and encourage the Natural Child's expressions.

Changes take place slowly, and it will therefore take time for our society to fully know, accept, and appreciate the Natural Child within us all.

Social shoulds and shouldn'ts do temper that Natural Child within, but we do, after all, exist as a part of our social environment. If it's socially unacceptable for a man to cry in public, his need for social acceptance may curb his desire to cry. The expression of feelings that had traditionally been unacceptable is gradually becoming more and more socially acceptable. People are beginning to ask "Why shouldn't a man be able to express his feelings as freely as a woman does?"

Today adults who habitually repress their Natural Child may excuse their natural behavior by saying, "If I hadn't had so much to drink, I would never have done that" or "Well, you know what drugs do to me." Depressants or stimulants such as alcohol, marijuana, or other drugs may be used to excuse us temporarily from Parental shoulds or shouldn'ts so that we can become less inhibited and more in our Natural Child state. We all have the need to express ourselves, but some of us can achieve this state only through artificial means. Artificial joy isn't "natural." How much more rewarding to be able to give yourself and others permission to make your natural Child an integral "natural" part of daily living.

The more we choose to allow our Parent messages to control us, the less natural and the more adaptive we become. In TA the adaptive Child is the "good little girl" or the "good little boy" who has chosen to conform to internal Parental controls. External controls are typically not obeyed unless they are internalized. In our attempt to please others we often go so far as to lose our own identity and ability to think for ourselves. If as children we fear that we are loved only when we "behave" or adapt, we may grow into adults who continue to behave or adapt in order to be loved.

What may have been appropriate survival behavior for you as a child may be preventing the emergence of your full potential as an adult. As a child you may have learned that, in order to avoid punishment or rejection, you could choose to play it safe and do what you were told. In your adult life you may still be "playing it safe."

Adaptive qualities are important and even necessary in our relationships with others because they are the "give" in the "give and take" in our relationships. If we attempt, however, to please all the people all the time, we lose our identity and simply allow ourselves to become mirror images of those who happen to be with us at any given point in time.

As children, we do not readily give up our natural selves. Our parent figures attempted either to force or gently coax what they considered undesirable, natural qualities out of existence. In our attempt to hold on to that natural part of ourselves, we may become quite creative in making others feel like "they are getting what they want while behind the scenes we are actually getting what we want." TA calls this creative part of us the Little Professor. Your Little Professor may have learned how to do one thing while "they" were looking and another when "they" were not looking. You may have learned to distort the truth in order to let "them" hear what "they" wanted to hear. You may have learned how to make others feel responsible for your shortcomings and how to get the kind of attention you wanted. The ability to manipulate to protect yourself or to get your needs and wants satisfied may well have been the psychological survival mechanism that was most appropriate to your childhood situation. If your parents thought nothing of punishing you, you may have put your Little Professor to work to protect yourself from those punishments. If you went hungry often enough, your Little Professor may have figured out a way to get you fed. If they continuously ignored you, you probably figured out a way to get attention. The Little Professor doesn't attempt to choose between "good" and "bad" behavior. It merely does what it feels it has to do in order to achieve its goal.

The Little Professor who protected you as a child may still be relying on old coping strategies that may no longer be appropriate or necessary. To distort the truth, to be constantly on guard or distrusting of others, or to be living life defensively is probably not desirable. Using precious energy that could be put to more constructive use is wasteful. As an adult, you can give yourself permission to relax and ask for what you want without having your "expert con artist" at work all the time.

Although manipulative qualities are very much a part of your Little Professor, this is a negative approach to dealing with life's situations. There is a positive aspect to your Little Professor, and that is *creativity*. Being creative gives you a positive set that allows you to express yourself not only through painting, sculpting, writing, and the like but also through great ideas that may be more far reaching than your manipulative tactics. The people you deal with in life can detect the difference between manipulative and creative tactics. The first is often resented, and the second is typically respected. In either case you may not get what you want, but, if your goal is not to make enemies but rather to win friends, then using fair and straightforward tactics rather than manipulative tactics will be more effective.

Are you aware of your natural, adaptive, and creative natures? Are you aware of your dominant Child qualities? Because different situations call for different kinds of coping skills, all three Children are vital to your life. Whenever you allow any one to dominate your personality, then you may become too self-centered or too natural, too eager to please or too adaptive, or too manipulative and not creative enough, and thus wasteful of your Little Professor. The following exercises will help you become aware of your current Child ego state a· d how well it's functioning for you. Here again, if you find that you would like to make some changes, turn to the action plan.

Exercises

Individual Activity

This checklist is designed to help you get in touch with the three different Children inside you. Circle the numbers of those items that describe you. Let yourself respond to this list honestly and openly so that you can get a realistic picture of yourself.

1. I express my feelings and emotions easily.
2. I mostly repress, or cover up, how I feel inside.
3. I talk readily about my feelings.
4. I often fake how I feel inside in order to please or protect myself and/or others.
5. I like to come up with good ideas.
6. Typically, I let my feelings build up inside until I feel like I want to explode.
7. I like to express myself through poetry, painting, sewing, and similar activities.
8. I only express how I feel when it's safe to do so.
9. I am basically a free spirit without inhibitions.
10. I use tears to get what I want.
11. I have no trouble asking for what I want.
12. I have no trouble making others feel like they have abused me.
13. I usually do the right thing at the right time. My timing is good.
14. I like to work for special recognition.
15. I can set things up so that I get what I want when I want it.
16. I like to express my frustrations on paper.

Class Activity

As a group go back over each of the 16 items in the Individual Activity you've just completed and discuss what makes each item an "N" or natural child behavior, an "A" or adaptive child behavior, or an "LP" or Little Professor behavior. Label each statement with an N, A, or LP.

Now list as many examples as you can think of that would describe natural, adaptive, and Little Professor (both creative and manipulative) behaviors and the feelings that may accompany these behaviors. For example:

Natural Behavior	*Possible Feelings*
Telling it like it is	Power, vengeance, relief
Open rebellion	Vindictiveness, anger, relief
Dressing the way you want	Happiness, satisfaction
Standing up for what you believe in	Strength, assertiveness, victory
Belching in public	Embarrassment, apologizing

Now discuss the possible feelings that would accompany these behaviors.

Adaptive Behavior

Saying please and thank you
Wearing the right thing at the right time
Handing papers in on time
Giving a birthday present on time
Waiting your turn in line

Manipulative Behavior

Giving a present late and getting away with it
Arriving late for dinner, again, without suffering the consequences
Telling someone you're doing one thing when you're doing another
Breaking a date for the wrong reasons
Acting like you have no idea how you got yourself into a situation

Now discuss the consequences of being predominantly natural, adaptive, or manipulative. Also, give examples of situations in which it's OK or not-OK to be natural, adaptive, or manipulative.

Individual Activity

Go back to the 16-item checklist. Look over the items that identify you—those you've checked. What do they tell you about yourself? How do you feel about them? What would you like to change in yourself? What kind of a person would you be as a result of those changes?

Small-Group Discussion

Discuss the following questions and identify the Child who would be dominating each of the situations:

Do you tend to cover up how you really feel inside, and, if so, how do you do this?
Is it important to be assertive and to get what you want? How do you do this?
How important is it to you to please others? How do you do this?

Individual Activity

Make a list of the people with whom you spend most of your time. Focus in on each person's Child ego state. Is that person predominantly natural, adaptive, or manipulative? How does that person make you feel? Do you like being with that person? What does this tell you about yourself?

Individual Activity

What do you like to do? Make a list of everything you can think of—writing poetry, singing, dancing, painting, cooking, decorating, problem solving, entertaining, going to school, eating, and the like. Now comes the important part of this exercise. Becoming aware of what you like to do is one thing, but discovering why you like to do these things is quite another. Do you enjoy doing these things because you want to do them or because you're supposed to do them? Do you engage in an activity because your best friend, relative, or lover likes to do it?

Check yourself out. Put an honest "because" after everything you like to do.

Example:
I like to *cook* because *I've always believed that "the way to a man's heart is through his stomach."*
I like to *dance* because *it keeps me in shape, and it's glamorous to be taking modern dancing.*
I like to *go fishing* because *I go alone, and it gives me time to myself.*
I like to *play piano* because *it pleases my parents.*
I like to _____ because _____.
Continue with your own examples.

It's interesting to get in touch with the reasons behind what you like to do. What do your reasons tell you about yourself? Do you do things for yourself, for others, or for both? Do you do them naturally, adaptively, or manipulatively? Would you like to change some of the ways you spend your time? How? What difference would it make?

How about the things you do but don't like doing?

Example:
I dance even though I don't like to because *it's the "in" thing right now.*
I _____ even though I don't like to because _____. Continue with your own examples.

Class Activity

Each and every person has the option of using either the *creative* or the *manipulative* Little Professor in any situation. Imagine using both tactics to solve the following problems, and discuss the possible outcomes. Add your own situations to those suggested below.

1. You're in a bind. You've made a date with a friend for Saturday night, but you've just met someone who interests you very much, and you would rather be with that person on Saturday night. Here are examples of how your manipulative and creative Little Professor might deal with this situation: Your manipulative Little Professor may tell

your friend at the last minute that other plans have come up. (This tactic does leave room for guilt feelings or the chance to run into your friend with your other date.) Your creative Little Professor has patience and will arrange to see the new person at another time. Another alternative would be to tell the friend the truth and allow him or her to make the final decision.

2. You're in a singles' bar (or any other place with many single people), and you're eager to get away from the person you've just met because someone else has just caught your eye.

3. You ran a stop sign you didn't see and were caught by the police.

4. You're in a restaurant. You ordered your steak rare, and it arrived well done.

Identifying your ADULT

How well do you reason, or, rather, how well do you "compute data"? You do have a computer inside of you. This is the part of you that takes in information, processes it, accepts or rejects it, and stores it for future reference. This rational, emotion-free part of you is your *Adult ego state*. Your Parent controls, your Child feels, and your Adult reasons.

It's appropriate for your Adult to decide what will be in the foreground of your awareness and what will, for the time being, remain in the background. In other words, it can rationally decide what you're going to deal with right here and now. Whenever you are reasoning, this data-seeking, data-sorting part of you accounts for your Child's emotional data and your Parent's controlling data. When your Adult is balancing the checkbook, your Child may be feeling guilty for having spent too much money and your Parent may be scolding you for not having better sense. Having "better sense" or better judgment is the same as having a well-functioning Adult. In the case of balancing the checkbook, your better judgment (Adult) computed the fact that you were feeling guilty (Child) and that you were scolding yourself (Parent), but it chose to leave all that in the background and proceed with the task of balancing the checkbook.

"Growing up" means becoming aware of and developing your Adult. As a young child you begin to learn how to analyze your Parent messages and your Child messages. You begin to realize that it's not up to your Parent but to your newly discovered Adult to make decisions. This is when you start to "think for yourself" and to develop an identity.

The process of becoming an individual who is unique and different from any other individual requires that you use and develop your Adult. The more you use it, the better it becomes and the greater the trust to "take yourself into your own two hands." The process of "cutting the apron strings," taking responsibility for your own existence, and trying out new alternatives in life is your Adult's development process.

Perhaps the most profound time period for testing the Adult is the teenage years. Teenagers are known to rebel against authority or parent figures who live by seemingly outmoded values. They fortify themselves with "peer power" and pretty much do what's "in." In short, they discover the generation gap. What they're really discovering, however, is their Adult. For the first time they feel free to test and explore their own decision-making strategies. This becomes so important to them that they may even risk total alienation from parent figures to take over being fully responsible for their own lives. Their decisions may be inappropriate in many situations, but that's not the issue. The issue is that, right or wrong, they make their own decisions and establish themselves as individuals. This striving for identity may include not only being "faddish" but also protecting and upholding individual values.

How do parent messages that teenagers so vehemently discount as irrelevant and even stupid later become a part of their adult lives? Teenagers become adults who tell themselves:

"I should only speak when spoken to."
"I shouldn't let others know how I feel."
"I ought not spend my time and money foolishly."
"I'm stupid and good for nothing."
"I shouldn't stay out late."
"I should do what's socially acceptable and proper."

Teenagers invariably enter adulthood, and they adopt coping strategies that resemble those of the adult role models they had as children. They become like those they rebelled against. Perhaps this is due to the fact that they haven't learned alternative ways of coping as adults. Society expects teenagers to be different, but adults are required to "fit in" with the status quo or else continue to be social outcasts.

When teenagers grow into adulthood, their Adult is faced with the realities of earning a living, perhaps raising a family, and establishing a place in society. When faced with such responsibilities, the Adult typically reasons that "fitting in" is the most logical and easiest strategy to follow. This strategy, they think, requires suppressing the Natural Child within. The degree of suppression, however, varies for different individuals. Some people may even live two different lives that enable them to be "responsible" some of the time—for example, at work—and "irresponsible" when they're at home, partying, or on vacation.

Perhaps as teenagers and adults our decisions would be better if we took the time to make sure that we were operating on appropriate data. The Adult is only as good as the kind of information it has on hand. Increasingly, the ability to make good decisions isn't necessarily dependent on mass data collecting. As the old saying goes, "quantity doesn't necessarily produce quality." An English major may not necessarily always know how to write a personal letter, a psychologist may not necessarily know how to internalize what he or she can contribute to others, and a mathematician may not necessarily be able to prepare his or her income tax forms. The acquisition of good practical common sense is a life-long trial-and-error process. Dependable and usable data result directly from:

1. making a decision;
2. experiencing the results of that decision;
3. weighing the pros and cons;
4. deciding whether or not to store that strategy for future use.

When the Adult doesn't develop properly or when it malfunctions, you may need either a major overhaul or a minor tune-up. Let's take a look at the various ways your computer can fail to work properly for you. One way is to operate on contaminated data. Another is to become either totally or partially decommissioned and still another is to overpower your personality so that you become Adult dominant.

False or inaccurate information will contaminate the decision-making power of your Adult. If your Adult accepts either your Parent's prejudices and superstitions or your Child's fantasies as *fact*, then the decisions you make will be inappropriate for the true situation. For instance, the Parent may contaminate the Adult with:

"Women are inferior to men."
"All men are chauvinists."
"Children must be punished if they're to grow into decent adults."
"Turn back if a black cat crosses your path."
"Never trust anyone who is a member of a minority group."

These beliefs turn men against women, women against men, both against children, and all against black cats. They also turn people against themselves. Themselves? Yes. Because *everyone* is a member of some minority group. Blacks, Scorpios, Jews, athletes, the aged, teenagers, and college graduates are all minority groups.

The Child-contaminated Adult will accept childlike fantasies as reality and may operate on any of the following:

" . . . and they lived happily ever after."
"Father (or Mother) knows best."
"There is a simple solution to everything."
"Justice always triumphs."
"Money is no object."

Such fantasies may make it difficult for people to admit failure in a marriage, to try to make decisions without Father or Mother, to face problems that *are* difficult to handle, to believe that the good guy loses sometimes, or to believe that they may end up in the poor house. When other people try to help the fantasy-contaminated individual grow out of his or her ignorance or naiveté, it is often an impossible task. Those who rely on fantasies often find it difficult to accept reality.

Another aspect of fantasy is what you can happily and safely experience in your mind. Many individuals contaminate their Adult with messages such as "Don't fantasize, because that's dangerous—you'll end up wanting what you can't have" or "Fantasy may keep you from facing reality and that's bad." Your Adult can reasonably say that a certain amount of fantasy is healthy and appropriate, because living out something in fantasy can be just as satisfying and sometimes even more gratifying to your Child than having to deal with making that fantasy reality. And it is often a lot safer. Even Jimmy Carter could "lust" in his "heart," or in his fantasy world.

Contaminated behavior is bad enough; but failing to use our good sense and the ability to analyze that behavior is probably the most irresponsible and debilitating act we engage in. Richard Nixon destroyed his public image simply because he "knew better" but chose not to act according to what he knew. It may be greed, fear of others, or lack of self-trust or confidence or it may be sheer laziness and an "I don't care" attitude that bring us face-to-face with our "irresponsible Adult." Regardless of whether your decisions are, in fact, made by a well-functioning Adult, in most cases you'll be held responsible as if they were. You may be overwrought with emotions or caught up in proprieties, but, when you make a decision and act on it, others will more than likely assume that your "responsible" Adult is in control.

If your Adult can protect you from contaminated data and irresponsible behavior, it can also tend to suffocate or dominate your entire personality. If your Adult is dominant and doesn't allow your Parent or your Child to express itself, you may become a computer-like person who can't express or accept feeling and who ignores generally accepted behavior modes. This type of person hides behind an invisible protective shield that keeps the self locked inside and everyone else out. This results in loneliness and emptiness. Others may consider such a person boring, insensitive, and noncaring.

Your Adult determines whether you're happy in life. Everyone has ups and downs, but, if you're basically unhappy, then you may want to reconsider some of your decisions. If your Adult's decisions are controlled too much by your Parent, your life may be rigid and without pleasure. If, on the other hand, your Adult's decisions are controlled too much by your Child, you may be playing much of the time and avoiding responsibility for your life. Typically, neither extreme is satisfactory.

Do you have a good data base? Are you comfortable with the decisions you make? Are you prepared or afraid to use your "good sense"? Do you need to strengthen your Adult? The following exercises will help you find out, and, if you decide that you want to work on your Adult ego state, turn to the Seven-Step Action Plan.

Exercises

Individual Activity

Make a list of all your current responsibilities, including household, marital, financial, job-related, school-related, and social responsibilities. Do not state your responsibilities as things you *have or need to do*—that's stating them as Parent messages. Do not state them as things you *want to do*—that is, as your Child's wishes. Instead, simply state them as *what you do*. For example, your list might look like this:

"I wake up at 7 A.M."
"I arrive at work at 8 A.M."
"I attend classes every evening from 8 P.M. until 10 P.M."

"I study on weekends."
"I play tennis once a week."

Now go back and take a good look at your list. Be aware of the fact that every item listed represents a conscious Adult decision that you made. You may feel that you didn't have a choice in the matter and *had* to make one of those decisions (Parent influence) or that some of those decisions were made because you just couldn't live without them (Child's influence). Regardless of your Child or Parent influences, it was your Adult who made those decisions. Good or bad, right or wrong, you're responsible for those decisions.

Put a "P" in front of each decision that was influenced by your Parent and a "C" in front of those that were influenced by your Child. Now ask yourself these very important questions:

"Am I making the kinds of decisions that are logical and appropriate to my life, or am I working against myself?"
"Does my Child have undue influence?"
"Does my Parent have undue influence?"

Ideally, your decisions are "good" for you because they have been balanced between the input from your OK Parent and your Child. Let's use the examples already given to see how this balance works:

"I wake up at 7 A.M. because I have to be at work by 8:30 (Adult influence), because I should get there on time (OK Critical Parent), and, furthermore, because I like to get up at that hour (Child influence)."

"I attend classes every evening from 8 P.M. until 10 P.M., because I have to work during the day (Adult influence). But I really want that degree (Child influence), and you have to inconvenience yourself at times in order to get what you want (OK Critical Parent)."

"I study on weekends because I have to work during the week (Adult influence); after work I don't feel like studying (Child influence), and I should study when I have a clear and fresh mind (OK Critical Parent)."

"I play tennis once a week (Adult), because it's good for me

(Parent influence) and because I just enjoy getting out with my friends (Child influence)."

Small-Group Activity

Let's take a look at how your prejudices and superstitions may be influencing your Adult. In your group, give examples of prejudice and superstition and discuss how these are currently influencing you. Share with one another how they affect the feelings you have about yourself. Defend the prejudices and superstitions you feel are harmless.

Now do the same with your fantasies.

Identifying your
EGO-STATE PORTRAIT

All of our feelings can be expressed as we expressed them when we were children. We can also remain totally dependent on Parent messages as we did when we were children. However, we no longer are children. We have grown into adults, and it may therefore be unnatural to express ourselves exactly as we did when we were two or three years old or to stick to all of our old shoulds and shouldn'ts. As adults, we're capable of all those childhood feelings and dependencies, but we may feel more comfortable if we temper them with our Adult.

Extracting the best from each ego state will help you toward greater intra- and interpersonal balance. All of you is better than just part of you, or, as a popular poster says, "None of us is as good as all of us." Each one of your ego states has something beneficial to contribute to your total self, and the total personality consists of a balance among your Parent, Adult, and Child. Our goal here is to identify a well-balanced *ego-state portrait*, or the kind of cooperative teamwork that your ego states can engage in (see Figure 4-1).

To exclude any one of your ego states totally or partially from your personality is to deny the existence of certain parts of yourself. Total exclusion of your Parent means eliminating guilt feelings, shame,

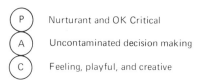

Figure 4-1. Balanced ego-state portrait.

and responsibility in your Child; thus you become a person without a conscience. Total exclusion of your Child means eliminating the feeling and playful parts of you; and total elimination of your Adult means losing touch with reality and possibly making your actions functionally inappropriate (see Figure 4-2). The varying degrees of exclusion of any one of these ego states will result in a corresponding degree of inappropriate behavior.

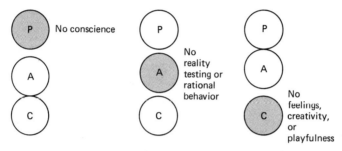

Figure 4-2. Degrees of exclusion.

Eliminating an ego state is the opposite of allowing one ego state to become totally or partially dominant over the others, again creating an imbalance in your ego-state portrait (see Figure 4-3). Individuals who are Parent dominant become preoccupied with social proprieties. They may also have a need to collect helpless and dependent people to spend time with so that they can play the role of savior. In addition, the Parent-dominant personality may have the need to be in a position of power so that he or she can boss, control, or persecute others.

We have already talked about the Adult-dominant personality, who typically comes across as dry and lifeless, and the Child-dominant personality, who can be so *natural* that it reverts back to raw, inappropriate childhood behaviors, so *adaptive* that it has no mind of its own, and so wrapped up in using its *Little Professor* that all of its energy goes into manipulative rather than creative processes.

The message should be clear: Too much or too little of anything is inappropriate. Eating too much ice cream can make you sick, and denying yourself ice cream every time you want it may cause you to become obsessed with it. Too much attention suffocates you; not enough starves you. If you study too much, you flunk out socially, and, if you don't study enough, you flunk out academically. The important thing is to find a happy medium. And that happy medium is different for each and every individual.

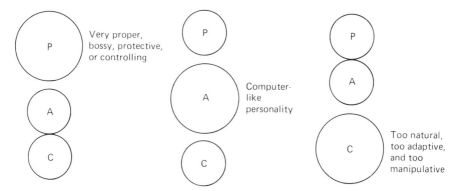

Figure 4-3. Degrees of dominance.

In addition to exclusion and dominance, we have looked at contamination, whereby the Child or Parent ego state has undue influence on the Adult's decision-making process (see Figure 4-4). Contamination often goes undetected, since the boundaries between ego states are fragile and ambiguous. It's not uncommon to mistake calm and controlled Parent behavior for rational Adult decision making. And it may be hard to tell manipulative and sly Child rationalizations from an Adult process. Learning how to use the Adult to arbitrate your personality isn't easy, because it's sometimes just too convenient to allow your Child or Parent to fool you.

Now that we've seen how it can all go wrong, let's look at how we can put it all together to come up with a balanced, well-coordinated

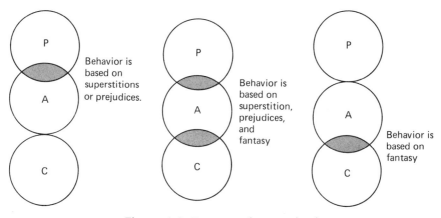

Figure 4-4. Degrees of contamination.

ego-state portrait. To achieve this portrait you will want to include your Nurturing Parent for comforting, the OK Critical Parent for keeping yourself safe, the Natural Child for expressing how you feel, the Adaptive Child for pleasing, and the Little Professor for expressing your creativity. In addition you'll want your uncontaminated Adult to evaluate the input from your Parent and Child and new data from the world at large before making rational and appropriate decisions. Let's look at how the team may operate to solve a problem:

Natural Child:	"I hate to get up early. I always sleep through alarms set to wake me up before 8 A.M."
Adult:	"The college catalog says the course I need is going to be offered at 8 A.M. next quarter and won't be offered again for two years."
OK Critical Parent:	"Take it!"
Adaptive Child:	"I really want to, but I'm afraid that, if I sleep through my alarm often enough, my professor may get angry and I may even flunk the course."
Nurturing Parent:	"Don't worry so much; you'll figure out what you should do."
Creative Little Professor:	"Joe mentioned something about directed readings, where you can actually take a course under a professor's supervision without attending classes, and that's a great idea! Maybe I can ask my prof to set up a directed-reading course for me."

Are you aware of your ego-state portrait? What are your helpful and destructive qualities? On a scale from one to ten, how would you rate your Adult's capacity to bring out the best in your Parent and Child and ensure that one doesn't overshadow the other or behave self-destructively? The following ego-state portraits are examples of different coping styles or personality types. Which one of these most accurately reflects your current "style"? How do you know that? Is there one that you would prefer to your own?

Exercises

Class Activity

Discuss the following well-known fictional and historical characters and identify their ego-state portraits. Support your reasons for saying that a character may be Parent dominant, contaminated, fantasy oriented, or balanced: Scarlett O'Hara; Martin Luther King, Jr.; John F. Kennedy; Hitler; Scrooge; Romeo; Macbeth.

Small-Group Activities

1. *Balanced Portrait*: Discuss what you feel it's like to have a *balanced ego-state portrait*. Identify, without mentioning names, people you know who seem to have a balanced portrait most of the time. How do "balanced" people behave? How do they cope? How do they live life?
2. *Exclusion*: In the same manner as above, discuss (1) people who don't seem to have a conscience; (2) people who seem to have a poor reality base and seem to lack rational behavior; and (3) people who lack feelings, creativity, or playfulness.
3. *Dominance*: Now discuss people who seem to be too socially conscious, those who are overly protective of others, and those who are bossy and controlling. Next discuss the computer-like personality. Finally, discuss the "too" natural, adaptive, and manipulative types.
4. *Contamination*: Discuss people who take on prejudices and superstitions as fact, then those who treat fantasy as reality, and finally, those who believe that both types of contamination are fact.

"What is my attitude?" 5

Identifying your
LIFE POSITION

It's not enough to say "All right, I'm going to balance my ego-state portrait," because without a positive attitude you may not get very far. A positive attitude consists of feeling OK about yourself and others, and in TA terms this feeling is phrased as *I'm OK, You're OK.* This positive life position or general positive attitude in life is the one that maximizes your chances to accomplish whatever you decide to undertake. The alternatives to the I'm OK, You're OK position are:

> I'm not-OK, You're OK
> I'm OK, You're not-OK
> I'm not-OK, You're not-OK

Let's take a look at each of these life positions so that you can identify your current position and whether you would like to change it.

I'm OK, You're OK

The most desirable life position is the I'm OK, You're OK position. The reason for this is simple. If you generally like and trust yourself and if you generally like and trust others, you will behave accordingly. You will treat yourself kindly and respectfully, and you will also convey kindness and respect to others. People are drawn to those who have a positive outlook; not only do they feel good around such people, but in addition they may be motivated to behave more kindly and respectfully. This results in an exchange of OK feelings and behaviors. When you're in pursuit of any goal, this type of self-support and support from others will more than likely make you feel like a winner—even if you don't reach every goal.

The trust element is perhaps one of the most important—if not the most important—factors that influence the decisions you make. Regardless of how well your ego-state portrait is balanced, if you don't trust yourself and/or selected others, then you diminish the quality of your decisions.

If you don't trust yourself or anyone else, then you eliminate two very rich sources of information. Self-trust means being able to recognize, understand, and accept the "good" and the "bad" about yourself. In addition it means knowing that you will make some mistakes but that you have the ability to get yourself heading in the right direction again.

Establishing a trust relationship with selected others means surrounding yourself with a team of friends who can help you check out your ideas. Such a group can expose you to a variety of alternative ways of doing things that might otherwise have remained unknown to you. Collecting as much data as possible prior to making a decision will enrich your data base and enhance the quality of the decisions you make. Entering into a cooperative effort with a group of people you trust to check out the ramifications of a situation is an excellent way of taking care of yourself and being good to yourself. The idea here is not to abdicate to the opinion of others or become dependent on them to make your decisions for you but, rather, to integrate the input from your OK people (friends, relatives, lovers, counselors, professionals, and authors) with your own to come up with the best possible alternatives to choose from. Your own input data must include a clear understanding of your values, interests, needs, wants, and abilities. This open-minded approach will increase the chances that you will be satisfied with your decisions and consequently with your direction in life.

I'm Not-OK, You're OK

Little children see themselves as very worthwhile people and as the center of their world, but they may and do feel subordinate to and dependent on adults. They're simply not in control—the "big" people are. They generally see themselves as not-OK and the adults as OK. The more they hear "No, don't do that! You're bad," the more not-OK they feel about themselves. That little person who has adopted this not-OK self-image will logically strive to become just like those OK big people, and this is, therefore, the time in life when the child is most susceptible to Parent messages.

To become like the OK people is to think, feel, and act like them, and the *I'm not-OK, You're OK* little person will attempt to do just that. This I'm not-OK, You're OK stance emerges during a time when the Adult ego state is just beginning to develop, and Parent messages are therefore adopted without question. This attitude is consequently premature, but it is one that the child typically carries into adulthood. It would seem logical that once the child becomes an adult he or she would automatically decide that now "I'm OK." Typically, however, this doesn't happen. The common position among grown ups is the I'm not-OK, You're OK position. No matter how OK others may say you are, you still filter everything through your own not-OK self-image. If you receive a compliment, rather than accept it you may typically respond with "Who, me? They don't really mean that." "They are just being kind." "It was only luck. It won't happen again."

The typical developmental cycle then, from childhood to adulthood, is one in which the adult who feels not-OK about himself or herself raises children who feel not-OK about themselves who in turn grow into adults who still feel not-OK about themselves. Where are the role models who have adopted the I'm OK, You're OK position? If they're not readily available for us to copy, then how do we get there? If you consciously strive toward the I'm OK, You're OK position, then you place yourself in a very special and exciting situation. For it is rare to be able to carve out your very own and self-made interpretation of OK-ness about yourself and others. Aren't you curious to see where you might take yourself in your attempt to consciously adopt the I'm OK, You're OK position?

Not feeling good about yourself, or not trusting yourself, puts you in a dependent position. If you see yourself as not-OK and others as OK, then it's logical to assume that you would feel more comfortable in giving yourself over to the advice and guidance of others. Since the momentum of life requires that decisions be made, if you don't trust yourself to make your own decisions, you automatically force yourself into abdicating to external controls. To exclude yourself from making your own decisions is the same as not taking responsibility for your own life. In this position, not only do you have to give up taking credit for anything good that happens to you, but you may end up really believing that all good things are due to fate, luck, and/or others. You leave yourself in a negative corner just waiting to be rescued. If you have decided that others know best, then you have no alternative but to remain a follower.

I'm Not-OK, You're Not-OK

The *I'm not-OK, You're not-OK* position shows a shift from seeing all those big powerful people as OK to seeing them as not-OK. What happens to the 2- or 3-year-old who comes to this conclusion and carries it throughout life? The answer, again, is logical. Those big people who appeared to be protectors and providers may have ceased to protect and provide; instead they punished and rejected. Pretty soon the little one who has already accepted the self as not-OK isn't getting any help from those who seem to be helping themselves. All "they" seem to do is punish and reject, and, as a consequence, the child sees not only the self but also "them" as not-OK. The sad part about the I'm-no-good-and-you're-no-good attitude is that nobody is any good; life therefore seems pretty lonely and hopeless, and for some it is not worth living. People who commit suicide are typically in this position.

The individual who has resigned himself or herself to this emptiness and sadness and is allowing the self to be bombarded with not-OK-ness from all possible sides will more than likely not care about developing an OK Parent or an uncontaminated Adult. This person really doesn't see a way of "fitting" into society. Self-rejection and rejection of and by others is the name of this person's game. The not-OK Critical Parent is in charge, and the Adult and Child are pretty much decommissioned.

It takes energy to motivate Adult- and Child-like behavior, and this individual lacks the hope and thus the drive to energize the self. Usually individuals cannot reverse this seemingly hopeless position alone. If this person hasn't severely regressed into this position, he or she can be taught to believe that "it can be done," "I have the desire to do it," and to commit himself or herself to a lifetime of getting there. The concept of "taking a lifetime to get there" isn't a negative one; one doesn't jump from one position to another but, rather, slowly evolves from one to another. Emerging into OK-ness gradually is better than remaining in not-OK-ness.

I'm OK, You're Not-OK

If the child who is in the I'm not-OK, You're not-OK position is not merely rejected but, in addition, is continuously brutalized, he or she may suddenly wake up and realize that I'm OK only if I stay away from all those not-OK people. This awareness creates new energy. Unfortunately this energy can emerge in the form of hate, resentment, feelings of revenge, and behavior designed to consciously hurt others. But of course there are degrees of feeling *I'm OK, You're not-OK,* and a less severe form of this position is the Parent-dominant type—for example, a nagging mother who believes that she's OK but her husband and children are not. She therefore feels that she has the right to nag, criticize, and force them to behave the way she wants them to behave.

The I'm OK, You're not-OK type sees no choice but to become very self-centered and protective of his or her own life space. Defensiveness and lack of trust of others become habit, and it is, therefore, not very likely that the individual in this position will adhere to or even adopt Parent messages. The Parent ego state typically remains underdeveloped. The extreme case is the individual who seems to lack a conscience and to be incapable of feeling guilt, shame, responsibility, respect, and affection for others. This personality will probably not hesitate to steal or even to kill.

Again, in the extreme case, it's not very likely that an individual in this position would ever allow himself or herself to get close enough to others to find out that people can be OK. And it's typically very difficult for others who care about such an individual to care for very long, because the average person usually gives up after so much rejection. Even the martyr may find it difficult to turn this person around. If, however, this personality is shown enough kindness and affection, he or she may begin to trust others and may therefore begin to adopt a You're-OK attitude.

There are plenty of not-OK role models around. Unfortunately there are not enough I'm OK, You're OK types to imitate. Learning about ourselves and others and how we interact may be the key to OK-intra-personal (within the self) and OK-interpersonal (between the self and others) communications. Understanding leads to knowing about I'm OK, You're OK feelings and behaviors. Such awareness can lead to adopting and activating this position.

Focusing attention on others means learning about and getting to know them and perhaps, as a result, helping yourself. We may be able to pick and choose our friends and spouses, but we can't usually pick and choose our parents, children, and teachers. We are therefore wise to learn to get along with different kinds of people. It is more difficult for some than for others, but we can actively learn about what it takes to develop and maintain respect, love, and friendship in relationships. This is a responsibility we all share.

It seems to be fashionable today to strike out to "find yourself" and to "do your own thing" or, in TA terms, to become "I'm OK." This goal is worthwhile, but it is incomplete when it's based on the assumption that others can take care of themselves and therefore don't need you. Taking responsibility for yourself and gaining a strong and positive self-image is insufficient if there isn't anything left over for others. Good relationships are based on mutual sharing and mutual positive regard. The goal is to share in mutual responsibility without feeling drained and "put upon." More often than not you may find that, when you reach out to others and give them some of your OK-ness, they will return some of the same to you. Rather than taking the stance "I'll take care of you *if* you take care of me," why not adopt the motto "I choose to take care of you, and when you learn to trust that, you may choose to take care of me."

In the I'm OK, You're OK position you can find peace within yourself and in your relationships with others. You can also give yourself the room to concentrate on how to enjoy life more fully and to comfortably share that with others.

Exercise

 The following small-group activity (four people per group) will help you to more completely understand and clarify each of the positions, to determine where you are right now, and to decide where you would like to be. Here again, apply the action plan in Chapter 10 to help you get there.

In this exercise each member picks a role—mother, father, sister, or brother. It doesn't really matter which role you pick first, because you will switch roles every five minutes so that everyone has a chance to experience each of the roles. Now that you've decided which member of the family you would like to be, pick a position. You can choose to be I'm not-OK, You're OK; I'm not-OK, You're not-OK; I'm OK, You're not-OK; or I'm OK, You're OK. Without letting anyone in your group know which position you picked, role play your position.

In your role-play situation you and your family can discuss anything—whether to go to the movies or what to have for dinner or any interpersonal problems that are typical of family relations. You may not even need to decide on an issue; just start playing your role and things will start to happen automatically.

After you've role played for the first five minutes, stop and see if you can recognize the position each family member adopted. Discuss how you know which position each person was in and why you reacted to that position the way you did. Was it what they said, how they behaved, what their physical posture was?

Remember to give each member the opportunity to play mother, father, sister, and brother. In conclusion discuss which position the father, mother, sister, and brother seemed to adopt most frequently. Did the mother usually put herself in the I'm not-OK, You're OK position? Did the father put himself in the I'm OK, You're not-OK position? If one particular position seemed to be a favorite for a particular individual in the group, ask him or her to try out a different position. It would be a good idea to make sure that each group member has the opportunity to try out not only the roles of each of the different family members but the four different life positions as well.

"How do I behave?" 6

Identifying your
LIFE SCRIPT

At one time or another we've all wished that we had the power to predict the future. In fact, we actually do have that power to some extent. We may not be able to predict what the world around us will do, and we may feel that we can't predict our own behavior. But somehow, when we do what we do, we're not surprised that we did what we did. Occasionally you may hear yourself saying "I can't believe I said that" or "I can't believe I behaved that way." You may surprise yourself with unexpected behavior, but generally speaking you can pretty much count on how you will cope in a given situation. How do you behave with parents, teachers, lovers, friends, and acquaintances and in group situations? How do you cope at home, at parties, at work, and at school and when you're out "playing"? If, for instance, you can say "I typically do things at the last minute" or "I'm typically shy and won't say much when I'm with a group of people," then you have identified some of your basic coping strategies. Unless you make a conscious effort to change how you behave, then you will continue using those same patterns in the future. You can, therefore, make predictions: "If such-and-such happens, or if I encounter such-and-such a person, then I will probably behave in such-and-such a manner."

Since the question "Who am I?" is answerable—that is, since you can look at your past and identify established and recognizable behavior patterns—then based on that information you can pretty much count on how you will behave in the future. That general picture you paint of yourself by using descriptive adjectives such as *shy, outgoing, reliable, wishy-washy, highly motivated,* or *lazy* is what TA refers to as your *life script.*

A life script is established in childhood. Children learn, based on how others behave toward them, how they must behave in order to

49

survive in this world. When Parent figures begin to shape and mold that Natural Child within, then the Adaptive Child and Little Professor begin to emerge in order to figure out ways to deal with these Parent messages. The child is fully aware of what's happening to him or her and thus begins to develop the Adult within who consciously accepts the behavior patterns that "work." Since the Adult isn't fully developed, the child has no way of evaluating whether or not these coping strategies are good or bad. The little person simply accepts whatever helps him or her "fit in" with the people and situations he or she has to live with.

Since childhood lasts long enough for any behaviors to become habit and since habits, regardless of whether or not they are appropriate, are easy to maintain and difficult to change, they consequently become a life-style, or life script. Although that script may no longer be appropriate once the child grows up, it's threatening for the individual to rewrite it. Habit is what is familiar, and trying out new behaviors isn't as safe as sticking to the old way of doing things. A child develops a life script with full awareness of how he or she interacts with others and the world, but a life script is usually perpetuated through life unconsciously. In order to change a life script in adulthood, it's vital that the adult adopt a conscious awareness of others and the world as he or she did in childhood.

A life script and a life position are not the same. A life script determines how you behave, and a life position reflects how you feel about yourself and others. One does influence the other, but people can have an I'm OK, You're OK attitude and still behave in a negative manner. You may generally like yourself and others, but you may not know how to help yourself and/or others out of failure-prone situations like not earning enough money to make ends meet, not knowing how to show love and affection, not knowing how to cope with depression, anger, and frustration, or not knowing how to be responsible. You may have an I'm not-OK, You're not-OK attitude and still manage to behave in a manner that is acceptable or that safely enables you to go your way and others their way.

A logical question here would be "If I want to change me, then should I work on altering my life position or my life script—that is, should I change my attitude or should I change how I behave?" Psychologists have pondered this question for a long time and have not come up with an "either/or" answer. The humanistic school of thought contends that an attitude change will influence a behavior change, and the behavioristic school of thought claims that changing behavior will result in an attitude change. It is, therefore, up to you to determine which you want to work on. The seven-step action plan will help you reach your goal regardless of which approach you want to take, for it allows you to work on your attitudes and behavior at the same time (see Chapters 10, 20, and 30).

You do have the power to rewrite your life script or to adopt a new life position. After all, you wrote the first draft of your script and developed your attitude when you were a child. Now that you are so much more aware of yourself and the world around you, just think of what you can do about your behavior and your feelings if you want to. Changing habitual behavior patterns and attitudes doesn't happen over night. After all, you have been who you are for as long as you have lived, and you will therefore need to pace yourself to grow into the new you gradually. You may even find it useful to go through "trial-and-error" periods; that is, you may want to try out new behaviors before you adopt them. Accepting the fact that it will take time for your new script and/or position to become habit will keep you from expecting too much too soon.

Even the world around us isn't standing still. When we look at our nation's history we can see how moods and attitudes have shifted. During World War II Americans typically saw themselves as "I'm OK, You're not-OK"; that is, Americans were united in fighting for what the nation felt was a worthy cause. Patriotism soared as Hitler and Nazism were being defeated. The war in Vietnam brought a different mood over this country. Americans lost faith in how the U.S. government was coping, and our population's general attitude shifted to "I'm not-OK, You're not-OK." We generally felt that we weren't coping with the world properly and that the rest of the world was not coping very well either.

Sometimes mood shifts bring about new behaviors and vice versa. We know from watching the mood swing of the nation regarding the proposed amendment for equal rights for women that attitudes can be changed in order to bring about new behavior. We also know that our society's behavior is governed by our Constitution, or the nation's script. Our courts of law and institutions of learning are constantly reexamining laws and the traditional way of doing things; they discard the irrelevant and implement what a constantly changing population deems valuable. Some 20th-century amendments to the Constitution include prohibition, the repeal of prohibition, the vote for 18-year-olds, and women's suffrage. When we look at the fact that the 1919 amendment outlawing the manufacture, sale, and transportation of alcoholic beverages was repealed in 1933, we become aware that certain regulations may not work and may consequently arouse a mood that causes new rules to be adopted. Change is growth; without it there is stagnation. We all have the ability to change; the key to effective change is not to latch on to what appears to be relevant but rather to look closely at a proposed coping strategy and try it out before accepting it. The ability to change, when combined with insight and understanding, is a vital process for nations, states, and individuals.

You are different from those who lived before you, and you are living in a world that's different from the one your parents knew. Perhaps some of the survival skills they taught you are no longer relevant, but that's up to you to decide. The decision to discard, alter, or replace a life script or life position is a very private and personal decision. What may be defined as foolish, timely, acceptable, or taboo by some people may be viewed quite differently by others. You are a unique person, different from and just as important as any other person, and what may be applicable to someone else may not be appropriate for you. You can decide what's good for you, and you can impose that good on yourself.

Exercises

Individual Activity

In order to gain a better understanding of your life script, make a list of adjectives that describe how you generally behave when you're with men, women, children, parents, and authority figures such as your bosses and teachers. How about with one friend, as opposed to a group of friends, or with one stranger as opposed to a room full of strangers? Now look at your list and answer the following questions:

1. What have I learned about myself?
2. In what situations would I like to behave differently?
3. How would I like to behave as opposed to how I am behaving?
4. Do I want to take on the responsibility of changing the behaviors I don't like? (If you do, the seven-step action plan in Chapter 10 will help you do that.)

Class Discussion or Small-Group Activity

Discuss the scripts society as a whole has imposed on us, such as stereotypical sex-role behavior, the impact of the mass media, especially the advertising industry, and the apparent eagerness for people to latch on to "instant joy" through drugs, cults, and fads. What's happening to the family as a unit? Is marriage obsolete? How do you feel about the government encouraging you to have fewer children? You may feel that there isn't enough class time to discuss all these issues, so select what you as a group would like to "chew" for a while. Some of the other issues may fit into conversations outside of class.

Class Activity

Just for fun let's look at the part of your life script that dictates sex roles. Put the men on one side of the room and the women on the other. Now each group should tell the other how they should behave, what their place in society should be, and the like. Don't forget to give the reasons for thinking and feeling as you do.

When you're through, discuss what you've learned about your sex-role script.

Identifying your
STROKES

Why change? Why bother? What's there to gain from balancing your ego-state portrait, acquiring an I'm OK, You're OK position, and revising your life script? For those people who are basically content and happy—nothing. But for those who are not getting what they want in life, changing, adapting, or even compromising the self becomes inevitable. What is it that contributes to making us happy? What is it that most of us search for continuously? What we basically want is to be loved, recognized, respected, and valued in a genuine and sincere manner; that is, what we want are *positive strokes* in the form of verbal and nonverbal endearments. These include everything from saying "Hello, how are you?" to "I love you," from a smile to a passionate embrace.

Your Child is the part of you that requires stroking, and it is also the part of you that knows how or can learn how to take, give, and receive such recognition. The Child is the "feeling" part of you, and it is therefore through your Child ego state that you experience stroking. It is your Natural Child that feels the joy, hurt, loneliness, depression, anger, and trust that come through stroking. It is also that Natural Child that bursts into tears, jumps up and down for joy or rage at football games, and vindictively and unthinkingly strikes back and rebels against others. The stroke-hungry or stroke-starved Adaptive-Child type may say "OK, I give up; I'll do anything to get my strokes." Finally, the Creative Child figures out the tactics necessary for getting what he or she wants. The tactics may be negative or positive, but this Child, if present in the individual, will find a way to get stroked.

Positive strokes are the most desirable form of recognition. If, however, we either don't know how to get our positive-stroke needs met or are around people who have learned to withhold positive strokes, we'll try instead for *negative strokes*. Negative stroking comes in the form of physical and verbal abuse. When we can't get recognition through positive means, we'll only allow ourselves to be alone, unimportant, unloved, and unwanted for so long, and then we'll try out new ways of behaving until someone finally pays attention. We all want positive strokes but are willing to live with negative strokes because the only strokes left are no strokes at all, and that's the worst possible fate. TA suggests that, without psychological recognition via verbal and physical stroking, people literally shrivel up and die.

The child who sits and plays quietly will soon want human contact. If the child is recognized—that is, motivated and energized through a pat on the head or through verbal means—he or she will probably feel satisfied and will continue to create. If, however, the child isn't recognized until he or she has had to ask for recognition, then he or she will try out a variety of attention-getting behaviors that may include throwing toys, crying, or getting into mischief until someone pays attention. At this point the attention may be positive; more likely, however, it will be negative. This is when a child may begin to learn about satisfying stroke needs through negative strategies that attract negative strokes. If positive strokes are unavailable, then the child will do just about anything to get strokes, even negative ones.

Imagine the child who isn't recognized at all. No matter what he or she does, good or bad, loud or quiet, mischievous or creative, he or she receives no strokes. This child would have no choice but to feel that he or she doesn't count and will probably wonder whether or not he or she really exists. This stroke-starved child will not only feel unloved and unmotivated to live but will also not know how to love or energize the self, let alone others. How does one learn to give unless given to, to take unless taken from, or to receive unless offered to?

We've often heard that "actions speak louder than words." This may be true in many situations, but action without verbal support and vice versa may leave you and others unsatisfied. If someone shows you that they love you through nonverbal means and does not accompany that expression with verbal endearments such as "I like you," or "I love you," then the stroking may be interpreted as negative. It is the combination of positive verbal and nonverbal stroking that is the most complete and energizing expression of love and caring. This love and caring is vital to our well-being.

Thus far we have talked about exchanging strokes with others. Being totally reliant on external stroking or stroking from others may result in an individual who doesn't know how to take care of himself or herself. Knowing how to be good to yourself, how to entertain yourself, how to recognize when you need or want to be alone, and how to let others know that you now require time alone are the kinds of skills that are necessary in order for you to understand that there is a "you"—a private, very special you who is capable of energizing, motivating, and protecting the self. Respect comes through positive stroking from others. But being able to actually respect yourself and believe that you have earned that self-respect comes from learning how to provide yourself with physical and mental nourishment.

Strokes are awarded to the self and others both consciously and unconsciously. Sometimes you may not even be aware of the fact that you're saying "I like you" or "I don't like you" to someone. We can't be conscientious all the time, but to be aware of how you give, take, and receive strokes is to be aware of who you are and how you cope. We all give positive and negative strokes, and we sometimes consciously withhold strokes every single day. We respond differently to different circumstances and different people.

Gaining a better understanding of your *stroke economy* involves looking at your ego-state portrait, your life position, and your life script. Your ego-state portrait may reveal a Parent-dominant personality who lives by "You shouldn't show affection, especially physical affection, especially in public, especially in front of children, especially not to your son." Or it may reveal the Nurturant-Parent-dominant type who has the capacity to stroke generously and continuously. The common Parent message when it comes to giving, taking, or accepting strokes is:

> "Be polite and appropriate."
> "Don't hurt anyone else's feelings."
> "Don't be selfish."
> "Do unto others as you would have them do unto you."
> "Turn the other cheek."
> "Don't let anyone know that they've helped you or you may have to pay them back."

The Contaminated Adult will undoubtedly make poor decisions about giving, taking, and receiving:

> "Give only to those who count."
> "It's OK to get what you want any way you can get it."

"If they don't know any better, why should I care? I'm only responsible for myself and not for anyone else."

If you *do* know better, then why take advantage of others? Why not, instead, practice some self-control and help them out? You would probably appreciate the same from them.

Your life position reflects the kinds of strokes you feel you deserve and consequently strive for. It also reflects the kinds of strokes you feel others should get from you. The I'm OK, You're OK position goes hand in hand with positive stroking; the I'm not-OK, You're OK position will elicit behavior that demonstrates that "I don't deserve positive strokes from you, but I will accept your negative strokes" and "I deserve no strokes at all from you if you don't choose to give them to me. You, on the other hand, deserve the kinds of strokes you want from me. I'll do anything you say." People with an I'm OK, You're not-OK attitude typically will not accept strokes from others. The only strokes available to these people are their own means to self-satisfaction. People in the I'm not-OK, You're not-OK position have given up strokes all together. Here there are no expectations of others and nothing left to give the self.

In taking a look at your stroke script you may find that you would like to change whom you associate with, how you behave toward others, and/or how you treat yourself. If a child gets used to positive stroking, then as an adult he or she will select friends who are capable of exchanging endearments. If the child becomes accustomed to negative stroking, then as an adult he or she will feel most comfortable exchanging abuse and punishment. The child who grows up without having acquired the skills necessary to satisfy stroke hunger will grow into an adult who isn't capable of asking for what he or she wants in either a positive or a negative manner. Finally, the child who has learned to live with stroke starvation will probably, as an adult, select to be alone or to be with people who have learned how to withhold stroking.

Some people collect strokes much like they collect green and gold stamps from grocery stores. If they shop at a new store and get a new kind of stamp, they may feel that it's worthless. But they will collect the old familiar stamps wherever and whenever possible, because they have already filled many books and are too close to that payoff to switch now. Some collect *"I'm-a-good-person" stamps*, and others collect *"I'm-stupid" stamps*, *"I'm-helpless" stamps*, or *"I-don't-need-anyone" stamps*. According to Eric Berne, self-indulgence in feelings such as guilt, inadequacy, hurt, fear, and resentment are defined as a *racket*. When you have learned how to manipulate others to help you wallow in the stamps you're collecting, you have learned how to promote your racket and you've developed a stroke script.

Teaching yourself and others new stroking behavior takes time. Those who are not accustomed to positive stroking will not know how to accept it, and they may even discourage others from wanting to give them positive strokes. Those who have been stroke starved may express much anger and resentment once they start receiving positive strokes: "How come you didn't give me this before!" They'll come face to face with what they've been missing and may be hurting very deeply for themselves. They may not accept the positive stroking, out of resentment or out of fear that these strokes will not be around for long. It may take a long time for these individuals to develop the kind of trust that is necessary for them to accept positive stroking. The stroke-hungry types may want to look at how they have been avoiding asking for and/or receiving stroking. Looking at your stamp collection or racket may be helpful in figuring out where you are now and where you would like to be.

Happiness, contentment, satisfaction, kindness, and fulfillment are all achieved through the sharing of positive strokes and through positive self-stroking. Degrees of pain, loneliness, emptiness, depression, and discontentment are all a result of negative stroking or the absence of stroking. The more positive strokes are absent, the greater the negative feelings about the self and/or others.

Some people only give *conditional strokes*; that is, they have learned to award strokes for "if's"—"If you do what I say, I'll give you a positive stroke; if you don't, I'll punish you with a negative stroke" or "If I do what I'm supposed to be doing, I'll like myself." We have already seen that both positive and negative strokes are forms of recognition, and both can therefore satisfy recognition hunger. If you must play controlling games or be conditional, you can still use positive rather than negative reinforcement. According to behavior-modification specialists, positive reinforcement following a desired behavior will strengthen that behavior. When negative reinforcement follows a behavior that is not desired, the response is strengthened. The extinction of a behavior will occur if reinforcement, both positive and negative, is withdrawn. So, if you reward desirable behavior, it will reoccur; if you punish undesirable behavior, it also will reoccur. In effect, you reward it. If your strokes must be conditional, then why not reinforce desirable behavior in a positive manner and simply ignore the undesirable to get the results you want?

The opposite of conditional stroking is, of course, *unconditional stroking*. How do you stroke unconditionally? Don't we all operate on an "if/then" basis? Is it possible to give love to others or like them for just "being"? Can we say "I like you just because you're you" and live with the belief that others *are* good rather than expecting to *make* them good? It's almost impossible to find a human being who doesn't do anything wrong. But that doesn't mean that we have to be on guard just in case they misbehave. If we can expect people to "blow it" once in a while, then we don't need to use our love to manipulate them into perfection. Instead, we can focus on and deal with the specific problem or problems that need solving without belittling or punishing the individual. Remember, the individual wants to be recognized in a positive manner. To reward a person with love and respect, apart from his or her undesirable behavior, is to say "I like you because you're you, and this problem over here can be solved." This attitude liberates or "frees up" an individual. He or she can stop feeling guilty or preoccupied with what to do next in order to be loved. Instead, this person can devote time and energy to problem-solving strategies or decision-making strategies without "hang-ups."

To stroke a 3-year-old unconditionally is not the same as sharing *unconditional love* with adults who have a developed Adult. A child's world is very conditional; it relies on basic need gratification and cannot take care of those needs personally. When a child is hungry or is experiencing physical discomfort or danger, the adult has to come to the rescue. That rescue can be unconditional. For example, it's natural for a child to wet its pants. It therefore seems illogical for that child to receive punishment and conditional love for such behavior. Since we can safely assume that a child will wet its pants, we can treat the problem without telling the child "Bad girl, mommy doesn't love little girls who wet their pants." Sooner or later the child will naturally grow out of wetting, and, if it doesn't at the appropriate age, then there are "kind" ways of dealing with the problem. Behavior-modification specialists have taught parents how to isolate problems in their children and how to modify behavior without threatening the child's psychological well-being.

Once the Adult is developed, however, then we have the opportunity to deal with equals who can care for themselves as well as we can care for ourselves. This is when unconditional love, based on mutual trust, equality, open expression of feelings, shared caring and responsibility, and the right to disagree, can be developed. Have you been unconditional to yourself lately? Knowing what it feels like to get OK treatment will help you understand how it feels to others when you give them such OK treatment. If you start by giving yourself OK strokes and taking care of yourself, you can then gradually extend that to others. As your OK-ness toward yourself and others continues to grow, you will eventually find yourself in the I'm OK, You're OK life position.

This chapter has been about caring and loving. Have you given yourself and/or others positive strokes today? Were they conditional or unconditional? Does your stroking come from your Parent, Adult, or Child? How does your ego-state portrait receive stroking? Do your strokes come from inside of you, or are you basically externally motivated? What is your stroke position, and what is your stroke script? Would you like to change how you stroke? If you would, the seven-step action plan will help you. But first, let's look at the exercises that follow.

Exercises

Individual Activity

This activity is entitled: "How do I love me? Let me count the ways." Make a list of how you go about giving yourself positive strokes; that is, what do you do to take good care of yourself?

Class Discussion

What are some ways you take care of yourself that you can share with others and that might help them take better care of themselves? Be creative—think of some ways to help the self.

Individual Activity

This one is entitled: "How do I love them? Let me count the ways." Make a list of the three most important people in your life. Now make a list indicating the kinds of strokes you have given them during the past week. In addition, make a list of the kinds of strokes you have received from them. Also, make a list of the kinds of strokes you actually accepted from them—that is, took to heart. And finally, make a list of the kinds of strokes you actually asked for.

Individual Activity

Make a list of the *conditions* you place on yourself. Now make a list of the conditions you place on the three most important people in your life. What do you do to yourself and to them if those conditions aren't met? What exactly are these conditions supposed to accomplish? Is it possible to get the same results unconditionally? What Parent messages are involved in the conditional stroking?

Identifying your
TIME STRUCTURING

Between sunrise and sunset we busy ourselves with our quest for strokes. We fill our hours, minutes, and seconds with the kind of behavior that we hope will satisfy our stroke hunger. The most complete form of stroke satisfaction comes from what TA calls *intimacy*. Intimacy consists of I'm OK, You're OK relationships in which open, direct, honest, and sincere communications are perpetuated. Unfortunately, too many people have a Parent that tells them to be guarded and suspicious of others, and so they shy away from intimacy. Because stroke hunger is in fact a major driving force in us all and because intimacy is desired by most and achieved by few, most people engage in what TA calls *withdrawals, activities, rituals, pastimes,* and *games.* These are all behavior patterns that approach but avoid intimacy.

By looking at these common "assembly-line" or predictable behavior patterns, we can gain a better understanding of what we do that is supposed to satisfy our stroke hunger but instead leaves us feeling unfulfilled. We do this daily without fail and typically end up feeling the same without fail. How is it that we know what we want but fail to get it? In our attempt to clarify and understand how we use withdrawals, activities, rituals, pastimes, and games, we may be able to come to grips with what we're doing ineffectively and learn how we can change.

Withdrawals

We can be face to face or voice to voice (via telephone) with others but be elsewhere in our minds. Most of us have learned, as children, to escape or withdraw from boring or unpleasant situations through daydreams and fantasies. When we become adults, our fantasy world may not be as rich, but it does give us a place to retreat to when the here-and-now becomes undesirable. Stepping into the private world of the mind is a form of self-stroking that allows us at times to escape and at other times to get in touch with our creativity. For this is the rich and fertile ground where "good ideas" are found and the imagination stimulated.

Frequent withdrawals from problems or people may be indicative of boredom, an inability to cope with situations at hand, or a desire to escape someone or something. Such escaping may be quite damaging if you do it long enough, because it becomes habit and consequently part of your personality. Withdrawing in this fashion is in direct opposition to intimacy, which requires that you face and deal with each situation, no matter how unpleasant it may be.

Favorite withdrawal tactics, especially for adults, are the kind that allow us to live in the past or the kind that fill our hours with the anticipation of and rehearsal for things to come. Too much living in the past, in the future, or in fantasy gives us reason to ask ourselves: "What am I avoiding? What am I afraid of?" or "What am I escaping?" Privacy is something we all need to have as part of our daily, weekly, or monthly schedule. But continuous withdrawal, especially in the presence of others, is something that may need to be examined.

Activities

Jogging, reading, sleeping, eating, bathing, working, and going to parties are all activities that can lead to greater intimacy with the self or others or can actually be a barrier to intimacy, depending on how we *structure* them. Going here and going there, doing this and doing that, sometimes doesn't amount to anything beyond going and doing. Though scheduled for activity every moment of the day, a person may be stroke starved. People often ask "How come I'm with people all day long and still feel lonely?" The answer is that you may be scheduling yourself to avoid facing unfinished business with your spouse, children, employer, employees, teachers, or friends. Many people become actively engaged in doing things with others in order to avoid facing interpersonal concerns; sometimes they get involved in endless activities with the very same people they need to talk to. They can't talk then because they're too busy "doing things." Rather than "really playing together" many people just mark the time with others. Real playing results from combining intimacy with your activities.

We often hear people say "I can't seem to enjoy doing things by myself. I would like to get into doing things alone once in a while just to learn more about myself, but I immediately start to feel alone and lonely." It takes time to learn how to enjoy being by yourself. This is especially true if you're in the habit of looking to others to satisfy all of your stroke needs. Becoming acquainted with how to take care of yourself and entertain yourself means structuring your time to be alone for a little while at first, and gradually increasing the time. During your time alone, pay attention to your Child. Listen to it, and do what your feelings tell you to do.

Rituals

Rituals are "good manners." They dictate the right thing to say and the right thing to do socially. They are the Parent messages that tell us how to behave at work, school, parties, weddings, funerals, luncheons, and anywhere else people congregate. Rituals are habits that have been bred into us since childhood and require nothing more in adulthood than continuous and methodical repetition of "safe" and predictable behavior. Rituals require that the Adult ego state be decommissioned. If it must operate, however, then for "ritual's sake" it best be contaminated by Parent messages. Superstitions and "lady-like," "gentlemanly," and prejudiced behavior are all rituals that are handed down from generation to generation.

Many adults have learned to be satisfied with rituals such as "Hello, how are you? Nice weather we're having." Though often meaningless, these strokes are positive and better than negative strokes or no strokes at all. When humans began to understand what was required to become civilized, they discovered rituals. "Civilization" or ritualization as we know it today hasn't been a part of humanity for very long. Some of us are still predominantly uncivilized and therefore are social outcasts; others are too civilized and have lost our identity; and still others are right in the middle struggling to determine the degree of ritualization we want in our lives. Some of us have come face to face with situations that haven't been ritualized, and consequently we are confused about how to behave. This world is changing more rapidly every day, and a well-functioning Adult can help us establish rituals for new situations that have no Parent message.

Some children are raised saying grace before every meal, and others are not. For those who have grown up with grace before meals, it's uncomfortable to begin a meal as a guest in another's home where no grace is said; and those who are not accustomed to saying grace before a meal may find themselves reaching for food too soon. Rituals are confusing because this world has so many of them, even for identical situations.

Pastimes

Before a relationship becomes serious or meaningful, we engage in harmless verbal communications that in TA are referred to as pastimes. These include chitchat, cocktail party or waiting-room conversations, and also role-playing behavior, imitating such stereotypes as "prom queen," "Southern gentleman," "town gossip," "politician," and "snob." Pastimes can be intermingled with withdrawals, rituals, and activities, but, as long as communications remain harmless and emotion free, they remain in the category of pastimes. Once you begin to "take things to heart" and hidden motives begin to regulate behavior, then pastimes give way to the games people play.

Pastimes are a common form of low-priority stroking and include such things as parents' talk about their children, singles' talk about other available singles, and students' talk about course work. Time passes, and emotions remain untouched, but the hours, minutes, and seconds are filled. Although pastimes provide us with much social interaction and stimulation, they are mainly exchanges that don't count emotionally. Once there is a spark—that is, once a relationship triggers positive or negative emotions—then the parties involved graduate from pastimes into either intimacy or games.

Games

It's how we go about asking for what we want and how we go about giving, receiving, and taking that makes us either game players or intimate individuals. If communications contain hidden goals or motives or if manipulation is involved, then relationships are "game-y."

Insecurities, fears, the quest for power, and selfishness typically lead to game playing. People can come face to face with and accept who they are with a statement such as "I am feeling afraid and insecure. I'm not sure what's bothering me. Will you help me work this through?" Instead they prefer to play games like the blaming game—"If it weren't for you I wouldn't be feeling like this" or "It's all your fault,"—or the defensive game—"Who me? No, I'm not insecure. You must be feeling insecure and that's why you think I'm insecure." Games endanger relationships, cause misunderstandings, produce misery, and certainly promote distrust.

When people choose to play games, they cast themselves and others into roles. Karpman identifies three such roles and places them in a triangle (see Figure 8-1). The triangle works because *victims* need to be persecuted and rescued, *rescuers* need to save victims and punish persecutors (they may also seek persecution), and *persecutors* need to punish both victims and rescuers and sometimes also seek rescuing. For instance, a son may play the role of victim seeking rescuing from his mother because his father is persecuting him. The mother may try rescuing both her son and husband and may even look to her husband for some persecution. Finally, the husband may persecute both son and wife and also seek to be rescued by his wife. And so the triangle perpetuates itself. If there is no victim, then the rescuers and persecutors are decommissioned. If there is no persecutor, then what's left is self-persecution. If there is no rescuer, then the persecutor has free reign over his or her victim. In addition to becoming a persecutor, rescuer, or victim type, individuals can and typically do, depending on whom they associate with, play their games from the angle that seems most appropriate at the time. A woman may play victim with men, persecutor with family, and rescuer with fellow employees.

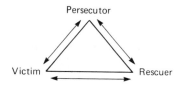

Figure 8-1. Karpman's Drama Triangle. From Karpman, S. Fairytales and script drama analysis. *Transactional Analysis Bulletin,* 1968, 7 (26), 39–43.

When the games people play are analyzed, it soon becomes clear who adopts persecutor, victim, or rescuer roles. We have all at one time or another played each of these roles, but, if we examine our "role" script, we may find that we have cast ourselves or permitted ourselves to be cast into one predominant role. We may have been playing that major role since childhood. To play our roles well, however, we must have the "right" games that attract the "right" players; then, if players are attracted, it is because they know how to play that particular game. Let's take a look at a few of the games TA identifies. We will look at the victim's, persecutor's, and rescuer's games and finally at those games that enable players to combine these roles.

The Victim's Games

1. *"Poor Little Me" and "Ain't It Awful."* The "Ain't It Awful" player, if he or she is in the Child ego state, may consciously or unconsciously seek out persecutors. This type of person actually looks for punishment and abuse, for the greater the mistreatment, the more there is to complain about. Here the role of victim also enables the player to slip into the "Poor Little Me" role. Both games attract rescuers. This game goes something like this: "Ain't it awful that . . . my spouse always yells at me, I never have time for myself, I can't go anywhere because of my children," and so on.

The "Ain't It Awful" player can also be in the Parent ego state. In this situation the player is the rescuer playing "Poor Little You." The need to nurture and protect the victim is an all-important mission in life. Unfortunately, this player only encourages the "Poor Little Me" player to remain in the role of victim; if there is no victim, then this player does not feel needed and may become stroke starved.

2. *"Why Does This Always Happen to Me?"* This player plays the same kind of game as the "Ain't It Awful" player but wears a sign saying: "Please don't kick me," which makes the urge to kick that person almost irresistible. This player typically says "Please don't hurt me" and invariably sets himself or herself up to be hurt. Or he or she says "Please love me" but doesn't do anything that anyone can love. The end result is an individual who continually complains "Why am I the one who always gets hurt?" "Why am I the one who is always taken for granted?" or "Why am I the one who can't get the kind of affection I want?"

3. *Wooden Leg.* The victim personality type thoroughly enjoys this game, which goes something like this: "What can you expect from someone who has a wooden leg" (or comes from the ghetto, is poor, stutters, has to study, is Black, is rich, is single, has to work all day, or has to take care of kids all day)? These people don't need persecutors, for they are their very own persecutors. They attract rescuers, but they will more than likely seek out other "Wooden Leg" players as companions. It's sometimes more appealing to wallow in self-pity in a group setting, with each member taking his or her turn, than it is to feel sorry for yourself all by yourself. The stroke value here is tremendous. The group that complains together may find a common complaint that emerges as a common cohesive cause to "fight" for publicly.

The Persecutor's Games

1. *"Now I've Got You, You Son of a Bitch"* (*NIGYSOB*). This player lies in wait for a victim. As soon as an opportunity arises to victimize someone, this persecutor will not hesitate to let out his or her frustrations. The persecutor will choose "Ain't It Awful," "Poor Little Me," or "Why Does This Always Happen To Me?" types to associate with. Those who play this game are typically in their not-OK Critical Parent or in their manipulative Little Professor state. This player may sound something like this: "I thought you were smart, but you disappoint me." "You always get yourself into trouble, don't you?" "You can't do anything right." "You're just like your mother (father)." "Why don't you grow up?" "I don't need you." "I don't understand why you're always complaining."

2. *"See What You Made Me Do."* This is the blaming game, which is indeed one of the most popular games played. It's always easier to blame others than to accept responsibility for your own behavior. The need to avoid blaming the self typically goes hand in hand with projecting your own shortcomings onto others and then punishing them for those shortcomings. Some lazy people pick on others, who may not be lazy at all, and accuse them of laziness and persecute them for that kind of behavior. Parents may spill a drink in a restaurant and immediately slap their child and state accusingly "See what you made me do!" The child may wander away from a preoccupied parent and into the middle of traffic. The parent rescues the child and blames himself or herself. The child simply feels "Why didn't you pay attention to me? See what you made me do?"

3. *"If It Weren't for You. . . . "* This persecutor teaches others how to become victim types or how to accept feelings of guilt. Actually, rather than a game this may be a form of *negative intimacy*, because what's involved here is direct, honest, open, and genuine expression of feelings. This individual tells his or her victim exactly what he or she thinks: "If it weren't for you, I could have gone to college, I could have been somebody, I could have gone on that trip, I wouldn't feel hurt, I would have gotten that paper in on time, I would have . . . ." Resentment, anger, frustration, and disappointment are fully expressed to this persecutor's victims. This not-OK Critical Parent typically shows no mercy. Rather than looking to the self for solutions to problems, this individual has instead learned to blame and punish others.

4. *"I'm Not a Loser."* Some people have a great capacity for making themselves the victims of their own persecution. These are the

individuals who refuse to accept or acknowledge failure or defeat. Regardless of how inappropriately they behave at their work, with their spouse, or in any given situation, they will not remove themselves from the scene. Instead they will "kill" themselves in their quest to try to "make things work out." Problem solving at "my own personal expense" to the point of self destruction is the name of this person's game.

The Rescuer's Games

1. *"What Would You Do without Me?"* These players compulsively seek out stranded victims and rescue them. They will attempt to create dependency needs in their victims, for the greater the dependency, the greater the need for that particular rescuer. The goal for this player is to create helpless individuals so that he or she can continuously remind them "What would you do without me?" This game can even be endearing—"How cute, you can never find your own socks" or "You have no sense of direction, aren't you glad to have me along?"

2. *"You Always Come First."* This is the rescuer who not only loves to put others on pedestals but also smothers them with affection and attention. The overprotective parent, spouse, lover, or grandparent may render his or her victim totally helpless and possibly unable to cope in a relationship in which he or she doesn't come first. These rescuers teach others how to take and accept but not how to give.

A Combination of Victim, Persecutor, and Rescuer Games

1. *"What You Don't Know Won't Hurt You."* This player may be hoarding information or lying to protect himself or herself and at the same time feeling like he or she is rescuing the victim with: "What you don't know won't hurt you." This player may also be a martyr who holds things in to protect others from painful news. Still others who play this game may tease people with "What you don't know won't hurt you" and thus accumulate much attention for the self at the victim's expense.

2. *"Why Don't You?/Yes, But . . . ."* This game requires a persecutor and a rescuer. The persecutor loves to find someone who is trying to help him or her solve a problem. The rescuer, however, hasn't got a chance, because the persecutor is quite skilled at coming up with reasons why the solution to the problem won't work. This game can last for hours:

Persecutor: "I have a problem."
Rescuer: (attempts to solve the problem) "Why don't you . . . "
Persecutor: "Yes, but . . ."
Rescuer: "Well, then why don't you . . . "
Persecutor: "Well, yes, but . . . "
Rescuer: "Then why don't you . . . "
Persecutor: "Yes, but . . . "

3. *"Look How Hard I've Tried."* Some people have a life script that has programmed them to fail. They actually enjoy failure, because it gives them the opportunity to lament their losses with: "Look how hard I've tried. Nothing I do ever works out." This individual may spend hours and hours working on a project only to have it rejected. He or she may spend years shaping a relationship only to be left alone in the end. A college degree may be sought but never achieved.

4. *Blemish.* These people find something wrong with everything. Everything is either too hot, too cold, too cheap, too expensive, too close, too far, too fat, too skinny, too hard, too easy, and so on.

5. *"Make Me!"* The "Make me!" players just love to get someone to tell them what to do and then can't wait to respond with "Make me!" People who get caught by a "Make me" player can't win, because, if they force that player into doing something, they are cruel, and, if they back off, they look foolish.

What we really want is intimacy, but, if we don't know how to achieve a state of intimacy, then we resort to playing games. The following exercises will help you understand more clearly some of the dynamics involved in the games people play. Your own games may even come into clearer focus for you. In selecting our friends we don't necessarily pick the most interesting or exciting people we meet; rather, we pick those who tend to play our games. It's helpful to become aware of the games we play; then, in order to eliminate games and create intimate relationships, we may need to look to a new circle of friends.

Exercises

Class Activity: Role-Play Situation

Select some of the games that have been described in this chapter, and have volunteers role play them in front of the group. Discuss what you learn from each role-play situation. Ask the players to express how it felt for them to be playing the game. (If you like, have them replay the same game so that you can try role playing in it.)

Small-Group Activity

This activity can be done outside the classroom. Select four or five games and discuss why people play them. What is their motive? What are they hoping to gain? Where does this game typically lead? (Be aware of how predictable the outcomes of these games are.)

Identifying your
TRANSACTIONS

As we have already seen, when people talk to each other, there is much more going on than mere lip movement and the exchange of words and physical expressions. What's really going on is that two ego-state portraits, two life positions, and two life scripts are communicating or transacting. *Transactions* are verbal and nonverbal exchanges between people. You giving me a message and me giving you a message represents one transaction. A conversation, therefore, consists of many transactions. Although the examples in this chapter will focus on interpersonal transactions, remember that transactions also occur within you, among your Parent, Adult, and Child.

Basically, predominant ego-state portraits, life positions, and life scripts remain the same, but each transaction may consist of a new set of ego states. Let's look at an example of how rapidly we go from one ego state into another.

Transaction 1
John: "I'm cold." (Adult ego state, looking for Adult response.)
Susan: "I'll turn up the heat." (Adult ego state.)

Transaction 2
John: "Apartments are all alike. No matter how much you turn up the heat, you still freeze." (Parent ego state, looking for Critical Parent response.)
Susan: "Isn't that the truth." (Parent ego state.)

Transaction 3

John: "Why don't we just curl up in this blanket?" (Child ego
         state, looking for Child response.)

Susan: "Okay." (Child ego state.)

These three transactions are not enough to provide us with the
clues necessary to identify dominant positions, portraits, or scripts, but
they do demonstrate how rapidly one ego state gives way to another. If
an individual is Parent dominant, this does not mean that the Adult and
Child are not a part of his or her transactions but rather that the Adult
and Child are mainly used to support the Parent-dominant position.
Transactions can be more clearly understood when they are analyzed,
and, to help analyze them properly, we can diagram them. Figure 9-1
uses transactions 1, 2, and 3 to illustrate how to go about diagraming transactions.

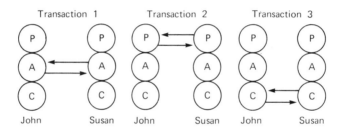

Figure 9-1. Complementary transactions.

These first three transactions were *complementary*; that is, each
response was expected by the parties involved. However, as Figure 9-2
shows, the conversation could have gone something like this and still
have remained complementary:

Transaction 4

John: "I am cold." (Child ego state, looking for Critical Parent
         response.)

Susan: "You're always complaining." (Parent ego state.)

Transaction 5

John: "No, I don't always complain!" (Child ego state, looking
         for Critical Parent response.)

Susan: "You just got through telling me for the tenth time that there are too many steps to climb to get to my apartment." (Parent ego state.)

Transaction 6
John: "Well, that doesn't mean I always complain." (Child ego state, looking for Child response.)
Susan: "Yes, it does." (Child ego state.)

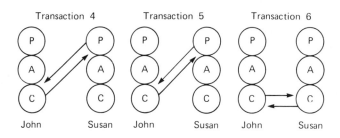

Figure 9-2. More complementary transactions.

If either John or Susan had been surprised with an unexpected response, then the transactions would have been *crossed* (see Figure 9-3 for a diagram of a crossed transaction). But since each responded the way the other expected, the conversation continued to flow in a complementary fashion. A crossed transaction between John and Susan would have gone something like this:

Transaction 7
John: "I am cold." (Adult ego state.) John is sending an Adult message and is expecting an Adult response, such as "I'll turn up the heat." Instead, John is surprised with:
Susan: "You're always complaining!" (Not-OK Critical Parent) Susan is directing her response to John's Child ego state. John feels confused and doesn't know how to respond.

Crossed transactions are conversation stoppers. John, in his attempt to uncross the transaction, may choose to stay in his Adult:

Transaction 7
John: "I am cold." (Adult ego state, looking for Adult response.)
Susan: "You're always complaining." (Parent ego state)

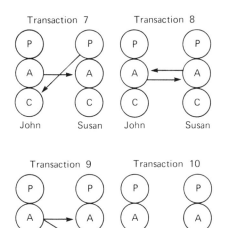

Figure 9-3. Whenever the vectors are crossed, as in Transaction 7, the transaction is crossed. Crossed transactions may be uncrossed, as shown in Transactions 8, 9, and 10.

Transaction 8

John: "I do complain a lot, but I *am* really cold. Would you mind if I turned up the heat?" (Adult ego state)

Susan: "You complain so frequently, and that makes me angry." (Adult ego state)

Transaction 9

John: "I would like to become more aware of when I complain so that I can stop doing it so much." (Adult ego state) John states a fact that seeks either an Adult or a Child response.

Susan: "How can I help?" (Child ego state)

Transaction 10

They kiss. (Both in Child ego state)

John's strategy worked. It might not have worked, however, if Susan, in Transaction #7, had succeeded in engaging John's angry or hurt Child (see Figure 9-4). It would probably have remained crossed:

Transaction 7
John: "I am cold." (Adult ego state—flat statement, looking for Adult response.)
Susan: "You're always complaining." (Parent ego state)

Transaction 11
John: "Get off my back. You're the one who's always complaining." (Hurt Child.)
Susan: "If we keep this up we're going to end up like we did last night." (Adult ego state.)

Transaction 12
John: "I can't stand it when you keep nagging at me!" (Child ego state—out of control.)
Susan: "John, you're not listening to me." (Adult ego state—statement of fact.)

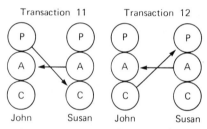

Figure 9-4. Crossed transactions.

Here John is obviously not getting what he wants. He wants Susan to fight with him. She refuses by giving him responses he isn't expecting. The transactions therefore remain crossed. John and Susan are not communicating with each other. Each one may as well be talking to the wall. Now, if John had hooked Susan into fighting with him, then the transactions would have been complementary, because the responses would have been expected by both.

In order to uncross a crossed transaction, one of the parties involved must start complementing the other. Complementing the other consists of behaving in an expected manner that may or may not result in a happy ending.

We have looked at complementary and crossed transactions. Now let's look at *ulterior transactions*, which are the kind that may appear to be complementary but that are in fact crossed by hidden and sometimes undetectable motives and messages (see Figure 9-5).

John and Susan's transactions could have contained ulterior motives:

> *Transaction 13*
> *John*: "I am cold." (Appears to be coming from Adult ego state—what John is really saying is "I don't like it here. I want to go to my place." He is actually in his Child ego state and does not want an Adult response from Susan. He would like Susan to read between the lines and respond from her Nurturing Parent: "Why don't we go to your place where it's more comfortable?" Instead, Susan, unaware of the ulterior motive, responds with:
> *Susan*: "I'll turn up the heat." (Adult ego state—flat statement)

> *Transaction 14*
> *John*: "No, that's OK." (Child ego state—John is surprised not to hear what he wanted to hear but still refuses to communicate directly and openly.)
> *Susan*: "OK." (Child ego state—playful) John is suddenly frustrated with Susan and doesn't understand why.

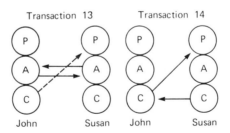

Figure 9-5. Ulterior transactions.

Every time you interact with others, you can actually diagram the transactions and identify withdrawals, rituals, pastimes, activities, games, or intimacy. You can also identify the kinds of strokes that are being exchanged. As you analyze transactions, it soon becomes clear whether you're interacting in a complementary or a crossed manner. In addition, ulterior messages and hidden meanings can be uncovered. It's interesting to note that complementary transactions do not necessarily consist of open, honest, direct, genuine, and spontaneous interactions between two people. They can, instead, be dishonest and calculating but complementary in that both parties know how to hook each other into response patterns. Games are kept going and become habit when transactions are ritualized. This will become clear as we look at the popular game called *Rapo.*

Rapo is a sexual game, played by both men and women. A woman may play the game by setting out continually to prove that she is a "good" girl, that all men are wolves, and that she also has seductive powers. She does this by hooking a man into her game. Once she hooks or victimizes him—that is, once a man actively pursues her—she delights in rejecting him. Men and women have played this game for many generations, and the transactions in this game are all complementary, because neither party is surprised by what is happening between them.

Exercises

At this point it might be helpful to get involved in some class activities that will help you figure out how to diagram and analyze transactions.

Class Activity

This activity is a role-play situation. It may be interesting for two class members to role play the game of Rapo so that the verbal and nonverbal transactions between the ego states can be understood more clearly. In this game what's suggested physically may be more important to notice than what is actually being said. Discuss and diagram the transactions.

Another game that may be interesting to analyze is the game of *Alcoholic.* This game clearly demonstrates how victim, persecutor, and rescuer types interact. The alcoholic is the victim who may select a spouse or lover who continuously persecutes him or her for drinking so much. Or the alcoholic may hang around people who are willing to play rescuer by providing just one more drink and recommending Alcoholics Anonymous just one more time. In any case, the attention the alcoholic receives centers around drinking and thus perpetuates it.

As the victim, the alcoholic sits in "center stage" in a life position that says I'm not-OK, You're OK, "You can help me if you try hard enough," or "You can really give me the kind of punishment I deserve for being so not-OK." The script is supported in that there are plenty of players who look for alcoholic types to play with. The goal is not to cure alcoholism but rather to play the games. The alcoholic's ego-state portrait will more than likely be Child dominant, because the alcoholic is typically in an emotional state, feeling self-pity or manipulating others into feeling sorry for him or her. He or she is also skilled in manipulating others to drink along or to buy the next round.

Class Activity

In this activity, you are to role play for about 5 minutes and then discuss what happened. First, ask three volunteers to play alcoholic (victim), spouse (persecutor), and bartender (rescuer). The alcoholic goes home, the spouse persecutes him or her, and the alcoholic escapes to the bar where he or she gets rescued by the bartender. Analyze the transactions (both verbal and nonverbal).

a. How could you tell which ego state dominated each of the three personalities?
b. What is each person's life position?
c. Does each support the other's life script?
d. What are the games being played?

In order to understand what's going on between you and someone else, analyze the transactions involved. Writing them down and diagraming them may help you in your analysis. The following is a dialogue between two people.

Carol: Every time I get ready to start studying my husband finds a way to interrupt me. He's driving me crazy. I don't know what to do.
Ann: Have you tried talking with him about it?
Carol: Yes, but he keeps doing it.
Ann: Why don't you study in the library?
Carol: I can't study in the library because I'm used to studying at my own desk.
Ann: Why don't you study when he's not home?
Carol: I'm not in the mood until after supper . . . .

Now see if, as a class, you can identify:

a.　The ego states in each transaction
b.　The dominant ego-state portraits
c.　The life positions
d.　The life scripts
e.　The game(s) being played
f.　Intimacy, if any exists

Class Activity

Now take a few minutes to write down a short dialogue between two people that you've recently heard or, if you like, one in which you participated. Take turns reading the dialogue to the class, and analyze it using the same format as suggested above. You may discover games you've never heard of before.

The ability to identify clearly what's going on between others and between you and others is the first and most important step in problem solving and decision making.

"How do I change what I want to change in myself?" 10

Identifying how to reach your goals: *A SEVEN-STEP ACTION PLAN*

This section of the book has made it clear that, in order to change yourself or make better decisions for yourself, you need first to know yourself. If at this point you have an OK understanding of your ego-state portrait, your life position, your life script, and the way you transact with others in order to exchange strokes and structure time, then you may be ready to undertake the Seven-Step Action Plan to bring about desired changes in yourself. It can't be stressed enough that a clear understanding of how you currently function is the mandatory prerequisite to undertaking a self-change project.

If you feel ready to commit yourself to changing certain aspects of yourself, then the seven-step change strategy that incorporates TA concepts will be useful to you. In addition to providing you with an easy-to-follow sequential strategy, this action plan has "built-in" self-motivators designed to energize you toward realizing your goal(s). These motivating factors are not gimmicks; rather, they require that you thoroughly understand how your current behavior is working against you and how your changes will be working for you. This gives you something concrete to reject and something concrete to look forward to.

The Seven-Step Action Plan

Before you undertake each of the steps, let's take a look at the plan as a whole.

1. Identify your goal.
2. Understand your goal.

3. Take full responsibility for reaching your goal.
4. Describe your action plan and set time limits.
5. Establish a stroke system to help you reach your goal.
6. Clarify how others will know that your goal has been reached.
7. Write a contract with yourself.

1. Identify Your Goal

Since it's easier to concentrate on one goal at a time, make a list of all the changes you would like to make and then arrange them in order of priority. Your list may include the desire to bring out more of your Natural Child, alter your position, rewrite your life script, or emphasize positive stroke strategies; to start, however, select just one of these goals. Since you typically interact with one person at a time and deal with one concern at a time, try not to spread yourself thin by taking on more than you can handle at one time.

Even though you'll be working on just one goal, you'll soon find that change in one area typically has a snowball effect and influences other areas. If your goal is to increase giving positive strokes, it shouldn't surprise you that, if you're successful, your position and script will probably be altered too.

Let's assume that the goal you have selected to work on first is to change your life position. As stated, this goal is rather broad and unmanageable. It's important that you restate your goal to make it operational or "action prone." To do this, clearly identify what your position is now and what you would like it to be and with whom—for example, "I would like to change my current I'm OK, You're not-OK position to an I'm OK, You're OK position toward my mother-in-law. Specify clearly "who" you're going to do "what" with and limit yourself to just one "who" and one "what." By narrowing your focus you will put yourself in a better position to understand the dynamics involved in the change process. In addition, you will provide yourself with a concrete example or "frame of reference" for future use.

When Benjamin Franklin undertook the "bold and arduous project of arriving at moral perfection," he enumerated 13 goals he wanted to attain and arranged them in order of priority, with temperance heading the list.

1. *Temperance.* Eat not to dulness. Drink not to elevation.
2. *Silence.* Speak not but what may benefit others or yourself.

Avoid trifling conversations.
3. *Order.* Let all your things have their places. Let each part of your business have its time.
4. *Resolution.* Resolve to perform what you ought. Perform without fail what you resolve.
5. *Frugality.* Make no expense but to do good to others or yourself; i.e., waste nothing.
6. *Industry.* Lose no time. Be always employed in something useful. Cut off all unnecessary actions.
7. *Sincerity.* Use no hurtful deceit. Think innocently and justly; and, if you speak, speak accordingly.
8. *Justice.* Wrong none by doing injuries or omitting the benefits that are your duty.
9. *Moderation.* Avoid extremes. Forbear resenting injuries so much as you think they deserve.
10. *Cleanliness.* Tolerate no uncleanness in body, clothes, or habitation.
11. *Tranquility.* Be not disturbed at trifles or at accidents common or unavoidable.
12. *Chastity.* Rarely use venery but for health or offspring— never to dulness, weakness, or the injury of your own or another's peace or reputation.
13. *Humility.* Imitate Jesus and Socrates. My intention being to acquire the habitude of all these.

He decided to make himself a little book and concentrate on one virtue per week. He recorded the "faults" daily and hoped to have mastered his goal by the end of each week. A blank space is indicative of no faults. (See Figure 10-1.)

Franklin's change process, though well organized, did not go smoothly. He experienced frequent relapses and at times was almost ready to give up. It is important to remember that the change process is not without relapse. If we drew a graph of our progress toward a goal, the graph would *not* show steady progress from start to finish. Rather, it would show a series of steps forward and relapses, as illustrated in Figure 10-2. Setbacks are to be expected as you inch your way toward your goal. Notice, however, that the new relapses never hit "rock bottom." Once you reach your goal, the end result should be that your new behavior occurs more often but not *always*. We human beings are simply *not* perfect. Benjamin Franklin put it this way:

"... a perfect character might be attended with the inconvenience of being envied and hated; and that a benevolent man

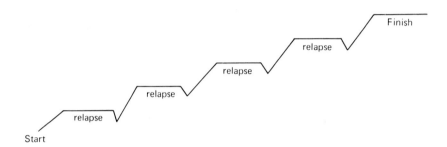

Figure 10-1.

	TEMPERANCE						
	Eat not to dulness. Drink not to elevation.						
	S	M	T	W	T	F	S
T							
S	✔ ✔	✔		✔		✔	
O	✔	✔	✔		✔	✔	✔
R			✔			✔	
F		✔					
I			✔		✔		
S							
J							
M							
Cl.							
T							
Ch.							
H							

Figure 10-2.

should allow a few faults in himself, to keep his friends in countenance."

He also said:

"On the whole, tho' I never arrived at the perfection I had been so ambitious of obtaining but fell short of it, yet I was by the endeavor a better and happier man than I otherwise should have been if I had not attempted it."

In a small group with three or four people, rephrase your goals so that they become clear and operational. During this process you may find that you rearrange your priorities.

2. Understand Your Goal

To identify your goal is one thing, but to understand the dynamics behind it is quite another. There are three basic factors that you must clarify before change will be possible. These factors are: (1) understanding what motivated you to behave the way you're currently behaving; (2) understanding what's motivating you to want to deal with this problem now; and (3) understanding what you're going to gain by reaching your goal. In short, you need to know where you are, why you would like to change, and how you will benefit from change.

It's important that you look forward eagerly to the profits you'll enjoy as a result of reaching your stated goal. It is this kind of anticipation that motivates you to want to act. In other words, you must adopt an OK position toward your goal. If you don't feel excited about what your new goal is going to do for you, then pick a more stimulating goal. This first goal may not be the most "worthwhile" goal on your list, but, if it "moves you," then use it. Otherwise you run the risk of not finishing what you've started, and you'll end up kicking yourself for not having been able to make yourself stick to it. The focus here is *not* on how it's all going to come out but about the process of "getting there."

Let's look at these factors more closely. If, for example, your goal were to change an I'm OK, You're not-OK position to an I'm OK, You're OK position toward your mother-in-law, then it would be important to clearly state:

What motivates me to behave the way I do toward my mother-in-law?
1. I feel she takes me for granted.
2. Her son is more important to her than I am, and I resent that.

3. My husband can't say no to her.
4. She seems to run our lives by manipulating my husband.
5. I want her to know she isn't getting away with a thing.
6. I want her to know that I am more important to my husband than she is.

What's motivating me to deal with this problem now?
1. I realize that it takes time for any mother to let go of her child.
2. I realize that I am tearing my husband apart because he does love us both, and it is unfair for me to turn this into an "either/or" situation—that is, love either me or your mother but you can't love us both.
3. I realize that I don't have to like her, but I can get along with her.
4. I realize that she is not taking my husband away from me but that I am alienating him from me.
5. I want us to be a family.
6. I want to make life easier on myself.

What am I going to gain by reaching this goal?
1. I won't have to keep up the barriers I've created (and that's hard work).
2. I'll gain self-respect by doing something I didn't think I would or could do.
3. I'll gain my husband's respect, because he knows how hard this has been on me.
4. I'll be able to take my mind off hating her and devote time to my school work and job again.
5. I'll be able to stop feeling "hurt" and sorry for myself.

Now ask yourself these questions about your own goal.

3. Take Full Responsibility for Reaching Your Goal

Not only do you need to identify and understand your goal. You must also take responsibility for it. Taking responsibility for your goal means being able to say: "I'm OK with this goal, and I want to reach it." You are the only one who has a complete picture of how your goal will change your life, and it's therefore you who must give yourself permission to pursue your goal. Whenever you find yourself asking others what they think or how they feel about your goal, you're asking for their approval. If they tell you that it is or is not a good idea, consider whether they really understand the situation as well as you do. You may want to talk to others who have had a similar problem to find out how they coped with the situation and whether or not a given strategy worked for them. This may be a good data base for you, but are they really in a position to tell you what to do? Typically they are not. It's therefore up to you to give yourself permission to select your goal, act on it, and take full responsibility for initiating your plan, carrying it through, and realizing the end results. Outcomes may be good, bad, or in between. We all want our efforts to end in success, but sometimes it's more important to try and fail than not to try at all. *Learning* can be defined as trying out something new. Without it we stop growing.

It's important that you make your commitment to your goal with an I'm OK, You're OK position and a balanced ego-state portrait. By taking full responsibility for your goal and stating that to you this goal is important, you've approached the situation with an I'm OK, You're (or it's) OK attitude. Making your commitment with a balanced ego-state portrait means making sure that your Adult has considered your Parent's restrictions and your Child's feelings and has weighed them properly prior to making a commitment to your goal.

If you make your commitment from a "rational" point of view only, without considering your Parent or Child, then you'll probably find yourself fighting against yourself, and you will more than likely not reach your goal. If you make your decision "impulsively" without considering your Parent or Adult, then you run the risk of hearing yourself say "I wish I hadn't done that." And if you make your decision because you know that it's "best for you," without considering your Adult or Child, then you run the risk of doing what you're used to doing and will probably talk yourself out of trying something new. You need a commitment from all parts of you. Your Parent can give you experience and wisdom, your Child can give you enthusiasm, and your Adult can give you the logic and order that will enable you to realize your goal.

4. Describe Your Action Plan and Set Time Limits

Now that you've clarified what your goal is and why you want to reach it, it's time to go ahead and act. This next step involves organizing yourself so that you can control your behavior. You need to state clearly what you're going to do, how you're going to do it, and what time limits you're going to set for yourself.

In our previous example of "adopting an I'm OK, You're OK position toward my mother-in-law," the following are logical mini-goals that will, more than likely, lead to accomplishing the major goal:

> *What Am I Going to Do to Make My Goal Possible?*
> 1. I will invite her to lunch (just the two of us).
> 2. I will call her just to chat with her.
> 3. I will smile at her more frequently.
> 4. I will talk with her like I talk with my good friends. (I'll add to this list as I think of more things to do.)

Notice that all behaviors are stated in a positive manner. Rather than saying "I will not say no when she invites me to lunch," say "I will invite her to lunch." And rather than saying "I would like to stop avoiding her," why not say instead "I will invite her to the house more often." Now it's time for you to state what you're going to do to make your goal possible.

Changes don't happen overnight. It's going to take some time to change what has become habit. This is not to say, however, that it's going to take you just as long to break your habit as it took you to develop it. When you were getting into it, you probably weren't aware of what was happening, but in changing it you are fully conscious and in control of your goal. You can set time limits for yourself. Initially your time frames may not be realistic, but with experience you'll be able to structure your time appropriately. Go ahead and experiment for a while until you get to know yourself better.

You have described your action plan and are aware that changes won't happen over night. Next you need to state specifically when you are going to do what and at what point you hope to realize some results from your new behavior. Your list of things you're going to do to make your goal possible might look like this:

> 1. I will invite her to lunch (just the two of us) *next week.*
> 2. I will call her just to chat with her *twice a week, and I will start tonight.*
> 3. I will smile at her *more frequently whenever I'm with her.*
> 4. I will talk with her like I talk with my good friends *every time I'm with her.*

Now set time frames with your goal. In order to determine when it's logical to expect some results from your new behavior, look over your action plan. Since you'll be talking with her twice a week and prior to that time you didn't talk with her at all, and since just the two of you will be going to lunch together, which hasn't occurred before, and since you will be behaving in a friendly manner, which will also be a first, you could probably expect results or at least a confrontation questioning your behavior within a short period of time.

5. Establish a Stroke System to Help You Reach Your Goal

Establishing a starting date and getting into your new "thing" is easy. It's sticking to it that's difficult. People who decide to start jogging, for instance, may start out running regularly for a few days but then find themselves unmotivated to continue. They somehow find better reasons to excuse themselves from running than to continue. How then do you set up a stroke system that will ensure success?

We have a tendency to do what feels good. And what feels good is not necessarily what's good for us; it's what's easiest and involves little effort and energy. This is why habits are not easily broken. To set up a stroke system that will motivate you to achieve your goal, you may need to use your habits as strokes.

If your habit is eating, watching TV, reading, working in your garden, spending money, or playing tennis, why not take charge of that habit? Instead of letting it control you, start controlling it. The goal is to not let yourself do what you like to do until you have done something toward your new goal. Don't let yourself watch TV until you've called your mother-in-law. Don't let yourself have your favorite meal unless you have invited her to come along. The longer you do your "new thing," the more habitual it will become and the less reinforcement or stroking you will need. Start out stroking yourself a lot. Then give yourself occasional strokes and eventually your new behavior will become habit.

Of course, it's up to you whether you use positive, negative, conditional, or unconditional strokes. Positive and unconditional strokes will be more enjoyable for you, but any kind of stroking will get you where you want to go. The key is to be in control of your stroking.

Go ahead and make a list of things you do habitually or things you like to do that you can use as strokes. Now select one of these to use in your stroke system. Next, identify the new behavior for that day that you will be reinforcing—for example, calling your mother-in-law and having a pleasant chat with her. Remember not to stroke yourself until you have done what you set out to do.

6. Clarify How You and Others Will Know That Your Goal Has Been Reached

What good is it to reach a goal if no one else knows that something has changed? In the case of adopting a new position toward your mother-in-law, if she isn't aware that something different is happening, either she may be unwilling to acknowledge you or you may have to do something that she can notice more readily. If she is actively rejecting you, then you will be better off to confirm it by "giving it all you've got" before you quit trying. Don't make the mistake of bombarding her with all your "good" behavior. Do it gradually so that she has time to get used to it. Otherwise, it will appear less than genuine.

If you've given it your best, how will you know that you've accomplished your mission? Here are some examples of how those who are involved in our mother-in-law example would know:

I will know that I have reached my goal when I:
1. think positive thoughts about my mother-in-law;
2. use positive statements with ease when I'm speaking with her;
3. feel good and not hostile when I'm with her;
4. do things for her without feeling resentful;
5. do things for her without being asked;
6. listen to her without jumping to conclusions.

I will know that my mother-in-law knows a change has taken place when she:
1. smiles at me and means it;
2. stops avoiding me;
3. stops hesitating every time she asks me to do something;
4. stops leaving the room I'm in;
5. hugs me and means it.

I will know that my husband knows a change has taken place when he:
1. says "You're really making an effort to be nice to my mother, and, whether or not she appreciates it, I really do";

2. says "I appreciate what you're doing; I know you don't like her, but I do appreciate your trying to get along with her";
3. feels comfortable and behaves that way when he's with both of us;
4. feels free to show affection to both of us when the three of us are together.

It's your turn to answer these questions about your goal.

7. Write a Contract with Yourself

Writing a contract not only pulls everything together so that you can have a clear picture of what you're doing and why you're doing it but also requires that you make your commitment in writing. Saying you're going to do something doesn't invite commitment the way writing down your intention and putting your signature on it does. You may want to support your commitment by adding the signature of a "witness" or "notary" to your contract. This may be a helpful step in that a cosigner such as a parent, spouse, friend, or child will: (1) strengthen your commitment because someone other than you knows what you're trying to accomplish; and (2) provide you with someone you can turn to for support and help.

It would be wise for you to form a support group of three or four members. Use this support group once or twice a week to check on each other's progress, setbacks, and problems encountered along the way. Also use each other for motivation, helpful hints and suggestions, and role models.

CONTRACT

I, _____, am making the commitment to take full responsibility for reaching the following goal:

I fully understand the factors involved in making these changes, because I can clearly state the following:

What motivated me to behave the way I do?

What's motivating me to want to change?

What am I going to gain from reaching my goal?

I feel that I am making this commitment from the I'm OK—the goal is OK position, and I have included my Parent, Adult, and Child in the decision-making process.

I will undertake the following new set of behaviors and set the following time limits:

What am I going to do to make my goal possible?

Starting Date:_____

Finishing Date:_____

I will use the following habits as a stroke system:

I will know that I have reached my goal when I observe the following:

I will know that _____ knows that a change has taken place when she or he does the following:

Your
signature

witnessed by

Conclusion

In this section of the book you were given the opportunity to check out thoroughly who you are. You looked at the rules you live by, your feelings inside, your decision making, your attitudes, and your interactions with others. If along the way you found that you wanted to change how you behave, you were provided with an action plan designed to make this goal possible.

As we progress through life things change. This first section gave you the opportunity to look at how you can better understand yourself and the world around you and therefore be in control of what you want to change. In addition, this section provided you with an action plan to help you reach the goals you set for yourself.

It may be valuable to reread this section or parts of it several times. You may choose to do this immediately or you may want to wait until the mood strikes you or an incident motivates you. Nevertheless, keeping this section close at hand to refer to may be helpful.

Now, if you're ready, Section II will help you look at where you would like to go—more specifically, at what you would like to do for a career and where that decision is going to take you in life. This section is appropriate for any age group: both 16- and 60-year-olds need to look closely at where they're going and whether that's a wise road for them to travel.

Section II

WHERE AM I GOING?

Sooner or later everyone faces the question "Where am I going?" This question has traditionally been the major issue for high school students, who had to decide whether to go to college, to vocational school, or to work. Their career choice was viewed as a lifelong commitment that would basically determine the life-style they would adopt. The notion that they might later find that career choice and corresponding life-style unsatisfying was used to stress the fact that the initial decision had better be the right one. Career changes late in life were considered signs of personal failure or of not having the ability to "stick to it." Mid-life career changes were typically viewed as a compromise; family members suffered embarrassment, "tightened the belt," and gave up hope for "things getting better."

Modern technology has forced many people who viewed life in a rigid and linear way to adopt a more flexible attitude. As machines replace people in more and more jobs, more and more people are forced to explore career alternatives in later life. In addition to those who were forced to change, there were people who grew increasingly concerned with questions such as "Am I happy?" and "What am I going to do about not being happy?" Statistics on current divorce rates and the increasing number of people who enter institutions of higher learning at age 28, 38, or even 58 suggest that more people are beginning to view life as flexible and cyclical. No longer is there only one right college-entry age or only one appropriate time to get married, have children, and buy a house. Traditionally, questions such as "Do I want to change careers?" "Do I want an advanced degree?" "Do I want to explore a different life-style?" "Do I want to get married?" were taboo in later life. Today they are expected.

The view that life is flexible and cyclical gives people the opportunity to realize that "the road not taken" early in life need not remain forever untraveled. Making "right" decisions for a lifetime has given way to making a "right" decision based on what is timely and appropriate. Today's rapid pace of living and increased life expectancy are enabling people to "get more living in." More and more people are expecting to experience major life changes every few years.

A timely or appropriate decision is a highly personal issue that requires the ability to pay attention to and understand who you are and where you want to take yourself in life. Section II of this book will enable you to explore where you are going. Although the question "Where am I going?" can be applied to a wide variety of life issues and should be viewed as an ongoing process in all facets of life, our focus here will be primarily on career orientation.

People do not stagnate unless they are not exposed to new experience. New awarenesses that may result from internal or external changes may confirm or validate that where you're going—career-wise and otherwise—is where you want to be going. Or they may make you realize that you would like to change your direction in your life. Growth can be joyful, but it is often painful as well. It's not a process you experience in solitude but, rather, affects loved ones who share your life.

In this section the same step-by-step format applied in Section I will be applied again—but with a new emphasis. When we looked at "Who Am I?" we learned to use TA concepts to explore the self. In Section II we will use the same concepts to check out where that self wants to go. Questions like "Who is controlling me?" (Chapter 1) will now be rephrased to emphasize our new focus: "Who is controlling what I want to become?" (Chapter 11). "How do I feel inside?" (Chapter 2) will now be rephrased as "How do I feel about what I want to become?" (Chapter 12). Each chapter in Section I will therefore have a companion chapter in Section II.

"Who is controlling what I want to become?" 11

Letting your PARENT work for you

Our rapidly changing world is pulling the rug right out from under many of us. No longer must we marry the match-maker's match, inherit our father's trade, remain confined to a particular socioeconomic class, or live out our lives within a ten-mile radius of where we were born. Our ancestors' blueprints for living have given way to new concepts about fulfilling our own potential and taking charge of our own destiny. Today, whether or not we like it or are ready to do so, each one of us comes face to face sooner or later with the freedom to choose.

Being in the position to choose freely how we want to shape our lives can be stressful and therefore undesirable. It's not easy to change habitual patterns in life, and the option to do so throws many people into a state of panic. Panic sets in for many reasons:

1. We don't know what's really out there for us to choose from.
2. We don't know how to go about finding out what's available to us.
3. We don't know what we want for ourselves even if we are familiar with our options.
4. Although we may know what others want from us, we don't know whether that's what we should want for ourselves.
5. We don't understand ourselves and our limits well enough to make appropriate decisions for ourselves.

So, even though we may have the freedom to choose, many of us feel unprepared to do so. To have this freedom and to fail to use it, however, can result in a lot of self-persecution later in life: "If only I had ..." or "If only I hadn't ...."

97

People whose lives lack personal significance are often easily spotted by their sense of indifference, sadness, and perhaps even bitterness. They typically seem to complain about how tired and bored they are, about how nothing they do seems to make any difference to anyone, about how too many strings are pulling on them, and about how they would rather sleep or watch television than do anything else. They may be the very people who opted not to exercise their freedom of choice to learn about themselves and explore alternatives in life that might have been more appropriate for them. These also include individuals who gave in to what others wanted for or from them. A lack of energy and motivation (or the opposite, which may include "work-aholism") is typical of people who have resigned themselves to carry out seemingly pointless functions in life. Such resignation often leads to feelings of insignificance and worthlessness, which are typically accompanied by a sense of powerlessness.

Understanding who we are and what we want doesn't automatically lead us to make the "right" decisions, but it does increase the odds that we'll make good decisions. If you took the time to think about Section I of this book, then you learned how to get to know yourself better. Your first step in that strategy was to look at the Parent messages that influence you. Now let's begin clarifying where you're going by checking out the Parent messages that may be influencing your decision-making process.

Do you recall as a child saying "When I grow up I'm going to be a . . ."? Whenever you talked about what you were going to become, do you remember describing and looking forward to what you would wear, the vehicle you would drive, the kinds of things you would get to do, the way others would see you, and the way you would see yourself? It was as if you knew exactly how stepping into that occupation would change your life. How did you find out about that career and about what it was supposed to do for you? Where did you acquire those Parent messages?

If you recall having had a dream about what you were going to be when you grew up, then you may also recall how your parents, relatives, older friends, and your older sisters or brothers reacted to that dream. Did they support you, or did they say something like "You will grow out of that. You should really do this or that, because . . . ." Did you grow out of your childhood fantasy? Did you accept the occupation that "they" expected of you? Or did you discard the occupation of your childhood dreams because "they" supported it and you wanted no part of what they supported? Regardless of how it happened, you are now in a position to reexamine your Parent messages, or the boundaries that you have constructed around yourself. These old boundaries, as well as your current ones, need to be checked out carefully, for they can either become your comfortable life-style or your entrapment. You can choose to tear down boundaries, keep them, or reconstruct them to better suit who you are.

Saying "I don't want to lead a meaningless life" does not help clarify what is or is not meaningful to you. While growing up we're bombarded with so many Parent messages telling us what we ought to want that often we don't know what we really want. As a result of "not knowing," we often allow values that are important to others rather than values that are important to us to control our lives. Let's take a look at how your Parent messages may be regulating how you think you should live your life.

Most of us are not faced with basic questions of shelter, food, and clothing; rather, we are fortunate enough to be able to consider "What *kind* of shelter do I want? What *kind* of food do I enjoy eating? What *kind* of clothes do I want to wear?" We have that freedom of choice, but that freedom is typically regulated by how much money we have. One set of values dictates that the more money you earn, the greater your freedom of choice and therefore the greater your happiness. People who hold these values may find themselves caught up in the habit of wanting. "The-more-you-want-the-more-you-get-and-the-more-you-get-the-more-you-want" is a self-perpetuating game that has no end. People trapped in this game are never satisfied or happy with what they have or achieve.

In addition to the money race there is the lust for power or title. The Parent message to "be somebody" is a driving force in many people. Once achieved, power or title is supposed to be accompanied by happiness, fulfillment, and satisfaction. For many people, however, this is not the case, and it may therefore be important to find out whose idea it was in the first place to embark on this quest. Some people become so engrossed in the goals they "should" pursue that they forget to ask themselves whether they really want to achieve them. The self-image and self-worth of a person often get wrapped up in the question "And what do you do for a living?" After you say hello and give your name, it's typically expected that you tell what you do to earn a living. Who you are is determined by what you do.

People who undertake the quest for money, power, and/or title may be living with Parent messages that tell them: "You can do anything you put your mind to." "The sky's the limit." "If you don't take advantage of these opportunities, you're a fool." "Money isn't everything, but it's way ahead of what's in second place." This point of view seems to have no upper limits; if you adopt it, you can supposedly do and be anything.

In contrast to this point of view are the injunctions that insist that you "get in touch with reality." This kind of Parent message often means "Get in touch with your limitations." Limitations are physical, psychological, and/or socioeconomic handicaps that ought to keep you from identifying and striving toward certain goals. A person who has only one arm can choose to allow his or her physical handicap to be governed by either the not-OK or the OK Critical Parent. The not-OK Critical Parent may interpret reality to mean that a person with only one functional arm shouldn't try to be a secretary, pianist, mechanic, or surgeon, occupations that require the use of both arms. However, the physically handicapped can also choose to focus on what they *can* do. A person with one arm doesn't have to lament the fact that he or she can't become a surgeon but can instead look forward to becoming an ophthalmologist or internist, using diagnostic rather than physical skills. There are many different jobs to choose from, and it is therefore self-defeating to focus on what you can't do rather than on what you can.

Other injunctions, such as sexual stereotypes, also confront us with our limitations. The not-OK Critical Parent tells us that we must curb certain hopes, wants, and needs, because of what sex we are. Men are not supposed to become nurses, and women are not supposed to become doctors. Men are not supposed to become secretaries, and women aren't supposed to become lawyers. Men aren't supposed to want to stay home with the children, and women aren't supposed to want to succeed in the world of work. The OK Critical Parent gives you permission to become what you want to become, regardless of your sex.

People often conform to stereotypical expectations associated with their socioeconomic status. Personal orientations—or "where people are coming from"—often lock them into what they think they should expect of themselves. The poor often expect to live out their lives in ghettos and to work as maids and janitors. The rich feel that it is necessary to maintain maids and janitors; those in the middle live with the fear of becoming poor and are constantly striving to become rich. Statistics indicate that socioeconomic lines are not usually crossed by most individuals. We stay where we are accustomed to being. Limiting yourself to what's familiar rather than exploring what you want out of life may stem from not knowing how to set different goals for yourself.

This "not knowing" is perhaps our greatest limitation. People do break out of their traps and reach goals they never thought they could reach, but the prerequisite for such achievement is knowing about alternative goals, understanding thoroughly what the requirements are for achieving them, and then adopting a frame of mind that allows you to see yourself functioning in that new role.

Some goals may not correspond with your present capabilities. However, since your mind is very powerful, you can learn to expect what you really want from yourself rather than what you feel you should or shouldn't want from yourself. You can reconstruct your self-image and become that image.

Less obvious but perhaps more powerful Parent messages are those that indirectly impose inferiority or guilt complexes. These often go undetected because they are communicated through suggestion and manipulation. In the analysis of transactions these injunctions would be called ulterior. The Parent message that suggests inferiority manifests itself through an individual's belief that he or she doesn't have what it takes to succeed in this world: "Your father was no good, and you're no better than he is" or "Be serious, girl, and don't go around thinking that you're cut out for anything special."

A guilt complex may be misinterpreted as family devotion or a commitment to someone or something. The "giving up of yourself" typically comes in the form of fulfilling "their" expectations of you or becoming what "they" could never become. Making someone else's dreams come true may be satisfying in the mere fact that a goal has been reached. It's unfulfilling, however, if that goal isn't also your own private desire. Some people don't feel free to pursue their own dreams until they have fulfilled their obligation(s) to others. Once this occurs, they may do an about-face and start living for themselves.

Your goal-related Parent messages may be helpful and supportive-OK messages or harmful and disabling not-OK messages. It's up to you to establish what's relevant and appropriate to your needs and wants. Clarifying the difference between the kind of life-style you feel you *should* want and the kind of life-style you actually do want is important. It's even more important, however, to understand your habits and realize that what you have habitually done for years is who you are, and changing who you are takes time and patience. If as a boy you became accustomed to your mother's not working, it may take time to adjust to living with a woman who chooses to work. If as a girl you learned to expect to be taken care of, then it may take time to learn how to take care of yourself and become the self-sufficient woman you want to be.

In the process of clarifying and identifying your goals you may want to call on your Nurturant Parent to help you through stages of confusion and indecision. You can relieve your frustrations and anxieties by encouraging yourself and giving yourself the strength to go on. You are responsible for taking good care of yourself, but remember that your Nurturant Parent can get out of hand. In becoming too good to yourself—that is, in giving yourself permission to take too many days off, miss too many deadlines, or overengage in self-indulgent pampering—you may decommission your OK Critical Parent's wisdom. Such behavior is usually called irresponsible.

We have seen that Parent messages may be driving us toward money, power, or title. We have also seen how they can block us, both directly and indirectly, from achieving our full potential. The direct messages confront us with physical and socioeconomic stereotypes, and the indirect messages are the ones that overpower us without our really being aware of what's happening. Both directly and indirectly you're bombarding yourself with both OK and not-OK Critical Parent messages. By checking those out and understanding them you may be able to clarify to yourself which goals you want to claim as your own. And as we mentioned earlier, rely on your Nurturing Parent to help you hurdle barriers, but don't allow it to overpower you.

Exercises

The following exercises are designed to help you become better acquainted with your three goal-directed Parents, the OK Critical, the not-OK Critical, and the Nurturing Parent.

Small-Group Activity

The following exercise is designed to help you clarify what Nurturant, OK Critical, and not-OK Critical goal-directed Parent messages sound like. See if you can identify which Parent would make each statement, and explain why you feel that the statements are Nurturant, OK Critical, or not-OK Critical.

1. "Go ahead, you can do it!"
2. "Yes, that was a dumb decision to make, but we all make dumb decisions once in a while."

3. "Why bother? You're not going to make it anyway."
4. "You should have a clear understanding of where you're going before you take your first step."
5. "That's OK, you can sleep in. You deserve it."
6. "It doesn't matter what you choose to become as long as you make lots of money."
7. "Girls should become secretaries, nurses, or elementary school teachers and not mess with 'men-type' jobs."
8. "Think before you make a decision, and take your time doing it."
9. "You can do it."
10. "Face it, your past history indicates that you probably won't amount to anything."
11. "Give yourself another chance."
12. "You should be the one who chooses what you will become, because you're the one who will have to live with that decision on a day-to-day basis."
13. "Don't waste your time with people who can't help you get to the top."
14. "You should have a clear picture of what is realistically possible for you to achieve."
15. "You can do anything you set your mind to do."
16. "Try not to make the same mistakes your parents, friends, or spouse made."
17. "Crush anyone who gets in your way of getting what you want."
18. "Don't think about it. Just do it."
19. "Work and pleasure don't go together."
20. "A penny saved is a penny earned."
21. "What you work for is what you deserve."
22. "Don't do anything you can't tell your mother about."
23. "You know that we know what's best for you."
24. "You can't just go out on your own."
25. "What makes you think that you're going to succeed?"

The following is how one class labeled these Parent messages:

1. N (Nurturant Parent)
2. N
3. not-OK (not-OK Critical Parent)
4. OK (OK Critical Parent)

5. N
6. not-OK
7. not-OK
8. OK
9. N
10. not-OK
11. N and OK
12. OK
13. not-OK
14. OK but could be not-OK
15. OK and N
16. OK
17. not-OK
18. either OK, not-OK, or N
19. not-OK
20. OK
21. OK
22. OK and not-OK
23. not-OK
24. not-OK
25. not-OK

Class Activity: Role-Play Situation and Discussion

The role-play situation involves a father and mother who are telling their 18-year-old son, who wants to play in a rock-and-roll band, what a productive work life and acceptable life-style for him would be. More specifically, they are telling him what his career should be (a doctor), where to go to school, and what kind of girls he should or shouldn't date.

Now replace the son with a daughter who wants to become a doctor; her father and mother are trying to talk her into taking on something more "practical" such as nursing or teaching. Discuss the following questions.

1. What were the goal-directed not-OK Critical Parent messages? How did they make the son or daughter feel? Check this out with the individual who role played the son or daughter.
2. Now do the same with the OK Critical Parent messages.
3. Did you hear any Parent messages that may have confused the son or daughter to the point where making his or her

own decisions became more difficult and perhaps even painful? What were they?

Small-Group Activity

Discuss the goal-directed Parent messages that have been confusing you personally. Perhaps you can attempt to clarify the difference between what others seem to want from you and what you want from and for yourself.

Individual Activity: A Questionnaire

Focus back on your childhood experiences, and answer the following questions:

1. Your ambition in life was to become a(an) _____.
2. When did you first decide to become this?
3. Who in your family, other than you, thought this should be your vocational choice?
4. What made you think that they wanted it for you?
5. What reasons did they give to support that choice?
6. What are your current reasons that support that choice?
7. How do your reasons compare with their reasons?
8. When was money put aside for your college education?
9. How did you know that?
10. How did that influence your career choice?
11. How did your peers feel about your career choice?
12. Are any of them entering the same profession?
13. What do those you admire most in life do to earn a living?
14. How does that compare with what you want to become?
15. Is there a currently "in" occupation?
16. What's making it so popular?
17. Is this your vocational choice?
18. What do the answers to these questions tell you about yourself?
    a. You want to please your parents, spouse, teacher, or others.
    b. You will do anything other than what they want.
    c. You want to do what your friends are doing.
    d. You want to do anything that's different from what your friends want to do.

    e. You prefer being one of the crowd.

    f. You prefer being different for the sake of being different.

    g. You know that you have selected the "right" occupation for yourself.

    h. Other.

Having answered the above questionnaire, how would you describe yourself? Are you living your own life, or are you molding yourself to live up to an image created by others?

"How do I feel about what I want to become?" 12

Letting your CHILD work for you

How many times have you brushed aside your gut-level feelings as not very important? When it comes to clarifying career goals, your Natural Child knows exactly what you really enjoy doing and how to best spend your money-earning hours. Unfortunately, when it's time to select a career, the Natural Child usually is the last to be consulted or is overlooked as not very important. Somehow most of us have acquired the belief that earning a living and "fun" don't go hand-in-hand. Work is supposed to be grueling, and the more unpleasant it is, the more we deserve the money we have earned.

Few individuals are aware of how much of their daily life is actually work related. If you consider, for example, that out of every 24-hour work day approximately 8 hours are spent on the job, 2 to 3 hours are devoted to getting ready to go, getting there, coming home, and unwinding, and perhaps another 2 hours are spent thinking or talking about what happened at work, then almost half of your 24-hour day has already been devoted to work. If approximately 8 hours are allotted for sleeping, then there are only 4 hours left for other things such as hobbies, family activities, meals, chores, TV, pleasure reading, grocery shopping, friends, and studies. Friends, more often than not, are the people you meet on the job, and consequently weekend time spent with friends channels the mind to work-related conversations. When you stop and think about it, you realize that work is the center of most people's existence. Even the kind of environment you live in and where and when you go on vacation is determined by what you do for a living.

If, in fact, just that much of your time will be devoted to your world of work, then that's pretty important business. How you feel about

107

your work and as a result of having spent time at work will be reflected in practically everything else you do. Your personal life can hardly be kept separate from your work. It may, therefore, be appropriate to allow your Natural Child to guide you, by paying attention to your dreams, fantasies, hopes, wants, and ambitions. Also focus in on your hobbies or the kind of things that your Natural Child gets excited about. If you love to spend time swimming, boating, and water-skiing, consider exploring money-earning opportunities that are related to such activities. If you love to read, consider reviewing books for publishing houses, and, if you're into health and nutrition, why not get involved in a health spa, health-food restaurant, or sporting-goods store.

   The key to happiness on the job is to check out your Natural Child to determine exactly what it is that you enjoy doing. Then employ your Little Professor to help you figure out how to turn that into a money-earning situation. When you consider all of the different kinds of businesses that have sprung up recently—such as boutiques in the 1960s and physical-fitness centers, computers, and plant stores in the 1970s—then it becomes apparent how important it is for your Little Professor to remain alert to current trends. Employ your Little Professor's creativity to integrate what you like to do with what's in demand. Use your Little Professor not only to help you discover your options but also to "open doors" that may have been closed to you. Being good at something isn't going to be productive for you unless you know how to get others to notice what you have to offer. Your Little Professor can be employed to do just that.

   Determining what you would like to do and taking steps in that direction require that you also allow your Adaptive Child to help you. Money-earning situations require flexibility, and your Adaptive Child knows how to be flexible. The "give-and-take" part of you can make or break your attempt to succeed in the world of work. The notion of being happy on the job does not mean that if you do what you naturally enjoy doing you will be happy 100% of the time. Your adaptability to the unpleasant aspects of your work will ensure, however, that you experience joy and success on the job more often than not. You may not like everyone you work with and you may not like everything about your job, but your Adaptive Child can help you make the most of every situation.

   Knowing that you should use your Child ego state to achieve success and joy in the world of work doesn't resolve such issues as "But I don't know how I feel" and "I still don't know what I want to do." Perhaps what you're really saying is "I choose to ignore how I feel and what I want, because how I feel and what I want are in direct conflict with what's expected of me."

We may disregard our Child's wishes because, in order to make them come true, we would have to "displease" others or "convince" someone that what he or she wants for us isn't as important as what we want for ourselves. It's often easier to displease ourselves or convince ourselves to accept what we don't want than it is to displease or convince others of what we do want. If this is what you're doing to yourself, then you're internalizing what "they" want as your own Parent message and thus convincing yourself that that's what you really want without consulting your Natural Child.

When we persuade ourselves that we want what we really don't want, we confuse the Child within us. The other side of the coin is to use our Little Professor to manipulate others into giving us permission to do what we want to do. Whenever adults use manipulative tactics such as pouting, nagging, or pleading to get others to give them permission to do what they want to do, they have already given themselves all the permission they need to activate their plan. So at this point they're not really trying to get someone else's permission. What they're actually doing is making sure that they aren't rejected for doing what they want to do.

Your Child knows what you feel and what you want, and, if you choose to ignore it, sooner or later you will either rebel or simply give up hope and find yourself following a life-style that you neither want nor feel a part of. This, of course, is inexcusable if you know better. The goal is to recognize the Parent messages that confuse your Child's wishes, then proceed to accept the OK Critical messages that are appropriate and relevant, and combine those with the goals that attract and arouse your Natural Child's desire. If you eagerly anticipate a goal and have your OK Critical Parent backing you on that goal, then chances are good that you will reach it.

Exercises

Individual Activity

1. Make a list of all the jobs you've had. Include every one of them, even those that only lasted a day and those you volunteered for.
2. Go back over your list and circle the jobs that you would consider doing again and would even go through the

required training to get hired.

3. Now make a list of the jobs that your parents, relatives, and friends have strongly suggested to you.

4. Go back over this list and circle the jobs you would eagerly undertake.

5. Finally, make a list of the jobs you would truly like to have. Include those you fantasize and dream about.

6. Go back over this list and underline the jobs that your Parent messages have labeled impractical or inappropriate for you. What makes them inappropriate? Are you talking yourself out of something you would really enjoy doing?

7. Look at all of your lists and study them. Notice whether, somewhere along the way, you have experienced for a day or more the job of your dreams. Also notice whether the jobs you've had have been ones that "others" approved of. Or were they merely convenient? Which jobs would you like to find out more about? Which jobs would make your Natural Child happy?

Now look again at jobs you've circled on the three lists. Do the lists clash, or do you find that your job experience corresponds with what "they" want for you and with what your Natural Child wants for you?

Small-Group Activity

Share your list of dreams, fantasies, wants, hopes, and ambitions, and talk about how you could go about making them come true. Think of someone you know who has been able to achieve a vocational or personal dream; tell the group about that person, emphasizing what you know about how he or she achieved that goal. Don't just choose from among adults; consider children and teenagers who have achieved their goals as well.

Discuss the kinds of skills these individuals employed and whether you can see yourself utilizing them. Why or why not? What does this tell you about yourself?

"How do I reason through what I want to become?" 13

Letting your ADULT work for you

We're living in a society that emphasizes immediacy: instant food, instant credit, instant cures, and instant joy. When such concepts bombard us daily, we have a tendency to allow our Adult to become contaminated with the notion that we can indeed find instant need gratification and instant success in life through instant decisions. Then, if the results of our decisions aren't instantly gratifying, we become instantly disappointed. At this point we instantly jump into something else that is supposed to instantly rescue us from the displeasure we have experienced. Many of us allow such fantasies to contaminate our goal-clarification and decision-making processes, and we are constantly finalizing decisions prematurely. Are you aware of whether or not you have been setting yourself up for such disappointment?

Although spontaneity is an important part of each and every individual's personality, it may be out of place when it comes to clarifying main goals in life and making important decisions. It takes considerable time, effort, and patience to take a rational look at our abilities, needs, and wants, what's available out there for us to choose from, and which goals may be both desirable and worthwhile for us to pursue. Not to make a commitment to work patiently and diligently to learn about our options and to integrate them with who we are and what we want means becoming victims of our own haste and impulsiveness.

It's often alarming to find yourself in a position of having to select, out of endless options, the goals that will become your own. When your future is at stake, making the "right" decisions can become a monumental and overwhelming task. This is where your emotion-free and uncontaminated Adult can help you. Rather than supporting a plan based on premature goals that grew out of insufficient or contaminated data, you can plug in your Adult to help you develop a sound foundation on which to base your decisions.

In the process of collecting and processing data your Adult can fail you. You may find yourself accepting as a fact the idea that women should become school teachers, nurses, and secretaries and men should become doctors, managers, and professors. Such Parent contamination will narrow your Adult's scope. In addition, you may be operating on the concept of instant joy, thus allowing your Child to contaminate your thinking. Conversely, your Child may also have you believe that "Once I get that advanced degree (or once I become a lawyer or engineer), my dreams will come true and I will live happily ever after."

Becoming aware of what your Parent and Child can do to your thinking may put you in the position of fearing them both and thus rejecting their input. Putting all of your power into the hands of your Adult, however, may provide you with rational goals, but, if those goals do not commission your Child's enthusiasm or your Parent's support, then your goals will remain unattained.

Your Adult's power lies in your ability to collect input from your Parent and Child and combine that input with relevant new data to establish a solid foundation for decision making. Establishing such a foundation takes time. It's actually an ongoing lifetime proposition. All of your life you have been making decisions, experiencing the results of those decisions, weighing their importance, and then deciding whether or not to store them for future reference. Your current decisions are based on those stored data. To improve your data base requires that you train yourself to make a conscientious effort to give equal weight to your Child's feelings and your Parent's recommendations and to apply that wisdom when you're ready to try out new situations. You are the sum total of your past experiences, and who you become depends on how well you learn to build on those experiences.

Some people just "roll with the punches" and give up trying to have foresight and insight into situations. On a moment-to-moment and day-by-day basis, rolling with the punches may be not only appropriate but also necessary. Needing to be in control of every situation all the time can result in a lack of fun and friends. Among friends, control is a give-and-take situation, but, when it comes to making important decisions in your life, then it's vital that you be in charge. If your Adult is lazy, then you may have a lot of good data that you're not putting to good use.

Sometimes a lazy Adult is indicative of a fear of failure. If you don't make a commitment to something, then you can't fail. This attitude results in a life that lacks movement. Regardless of where you are in life, people will assume that you have consciously put yourself there. Since their assumption is that you are in control of where you are, you will be treated accordingly. Many people would be surprised to find out that where you are isn't at all where you want to be and that what you're doing isn't at all what you want to be doing. Since you're going to be held responsible for your situation, why not take control of where you are and what you're doing?

There are three stages to making a career choice: the fantasy stage, in which you daydream about it; the tentative stage, in which you try it out; and the concrete stage, in which you make a commitment to take the steps necessary to make it part of your life. Before finalizing a career choice, answer the following questions. You may find them helpful.

1. What's the occupation really like?
2. How do I know this to be a true and a real description of this occupation?
3. What's the required preparation?
4. What's it going to cost in time and money?
5. What do the important people in my life have to say about it?
6. What are the advancement opportunities?
7. What's the employment outlook in that field?
8. How will this occupation influence me on a day-by-day basis?
9. Will it require that I move frequently?
10. What is it exactly that draws me to this occupation?

If you don't know the answers to some of these questions, then you may want to check out some information sources. Books and magazines are a quick way to broaden your awareness. Every library has numerous biographical and autobiographical accounts of people who have succeeded in reaching their goals. In addition to these success stories, public or school libraries have some basic vocational guides. Feel free to ask your librarian to help you locate some of these sources. If you're fortunate enough to have access to a well-stocked resource center, be sure to use it.

You will be amazed at the many different self-help vocational guides that are available. Among them is *The Occupational Outlook*

Handbook, published biannually by the Bureau of Labor Statistics. This handbook is one of the most accurate and useful sources of occupational information. It provides the following information on over 800 occupations:

1. job description
2. training required
3. qualifications
4. advancement opportunities
5. employment outlook (whether the job is likely to be available when you're ready for it)
6. working conditions
7. salary

The Occupational Outlook Quarterly is a supplement that updates *The Occupational Outlook Handbook* four times a year. *The Dictionary of Occupational Titles,* put out by the Department of Labor, provides you with information on over 22,000 jobs. It groups jobs into nine broad categories such as professional, technical, managerial, and sales, and then specifies 22 areas of work such as business relations, medicine and health, art, and mathematics and science.

Printed materials may help you pinpoint what looks attractive to you, but what looks attractive on paper may not attract you at all once you talk with and watch the people who are actually doing it. So talk with people and observe them. Find out what they like and dislike about what they're doing. Check out the advantages and disadvantages as they describe them. Ask them what their expectations were *before* they got involved in that career. Finally, ask them to give you helpful hints about shortcuts, steps you can take to prepare yourself for the job, and their predictions about how the job will change over the next 15 to 20 years. Inviting personnel managers, deans of colleges, people working for firms, or self-employed people to talk with your class is another way to make contact and get helpful information.

Interest inventories give you an opportunity to check out your interests and to compare them with those of people already employed in a wide range of jobs. Getting an idea of how you compare with people on the job does not necessarily mean that you will be happy doing what they're doing. Interest inventories are not designed to tell you what to do. They help you check out your likes and dislikes, which may be a good way for you to start clarifying where you would like to be.

When answering questions on an interest inventory, remember

that you're not taking a test. There are no right or wrong answers. Respond to the items with how you really feel and not with how you think you *should* feel. The goal is to get a clear picture of what your interests are, and, when you get your computer-scored results back, you can take a look at whether or not you agree with how the inventory describes you.

What's especially helpful about getting results back from an interest inventory such as the Strong-Campbell, which is the most thoroughly researched inventory available, is the long list of many different kinds of occupations that can help you become familiar with what's out there for you.

Personality profiles may help you gain a better understanding of your behavior. They enable you to predict, based on your answers, how you will more than likely behave in certain situations. They give you insight into what is going on "inside" of you—your interests, attitudes, needs, and conflicts. And based on this information you can decide (1) whether or not you would like to change your behavior and (2) which occupation would be suitable to the kind of person you are or would like to be. Most school counseling centers have personality profiles and interest inventories on hand and can help you to interpret them.

Apprenticeships, internships, or practicums are probably the very best way of finding out whether you would like to do what you think you would like to do. Often, practical experience in a career-oriented program is left until the last semester or quarter in college or treated as something that doesn't happen until you actually accept a job. On-the-job experience at the beginning of your college career (or as soon as you find something you want to try) will help you decide whether or not you would enjoy sticking with it before you invest several years in preparatory courses. If your career choice looks and sounds good, why not find out whether or not it also feels good?

An internship at the very beginning of your occupational preparations will not only help you clarify whether you're in the right field but will also put you in touch with the very people who may be hiring you in the future or may be in a position to give you a good recommendation. It would be ideal, of course, if that internship or apprenticeship offered a salary. Even without pay, however, they can be worth a great deal. You may even want to create an internship, by searching for the "right" spot and convincing employers that you are competent and reliable and so interested in the opportunity to observe and experience your possible future job that you're willing to work for no pay.

Even after you have thoroughly researched what's available to you and selected what you consider to be your ideal goal(s), you can still trap yourself into becoming a loser rather than a winner in life. A loser's course of action is to:

1. know what you want but opt not to undertake it;
2. "give it a go" once and not give yourself a second, third, or even a fourth chance to succeed;
3. hold yourself back because of your age;
4. lock yourself into just one occupational endeavor, without the kinds of skills that can provide you with job alternatives.

If you lock yourself into only one way of getting where you want to go, you may someday find you've fallen short of what you envisioned for yourself in life.

Whereas the loser rejects self-protective strategies and thus fails to take care of the self, the winner ensures that:

1. all options have been considered;
2. more than one option has been selected as a security measure;
3. options have been selected based on input from a balanced ego-state portrait;
4. he or she will give himself or herself more than one chance to succeed;
5. age is not an obstacle to defining and reaching new goals.

Today's life expectancy makes it possible to start over again at age 40 or even 50, because the average person can expect to live to be 70 years old.

Exercises

The activities for this section are "go and do" individual activities.

1. Go to your nearest counseling center, either at school or in your community, and take a vocational-interest battery that includes a personality profile.
2. Ask one of the vocational counselors to interpret the results for you.

3. Don't allow your inventory results to dictate your career choice; rather, think them through carefully and compare the results with what your balanced ego-state portrait has selected for you.

4. Go to your nearest library and read about occupations that interest you. Check *The Occupational Outlook Handbook, The Occupational Outlook Quarterly,* and *The Dictionary of Occupational Titles.*

5. Find some books and articles on careers you're really excited about that give you an in-depth picture of the pleasant and not-so-pleasant experiences that the fictional or real-life personalities went through in order to reach their career goals and how they felt once they actually got there.

6. Find people who are currently employed in the field of your choice and make appointments to talk to them about that career.

7. Start thinking about when and where you might want to set up an internship or practicum for yourself.

"How do I currently make my vocational decisions?" 14

Letting your EGO-STATE PORTRAIT work for you

People frequently ask "What advice can you give me about how to decide what work I'm best suited for, how to do well in a job interview, and how to keep the job once I get it?" TA would encourage you to approach each of these situations with a balanced ego-state portrait and an I'm OK, You're OK position. This position will be discussed in Chapter 15; for now, let's focus on how a balanced ego-state portrait can successfully be applied to career selection, interview sessions, and job maintenance.

Your best career choice is one that your Adult has thoroughly researched, your Parent has carefully scrutinized, and your Child has eagerly accepted. This balance is not easy to achieve; it requires that your Adult continually negotiate among your Parent, Child, and the data it collects from external sources. Your Adult may compute that you should become an attorney. If your Child reacts with boredom, then that project is best abandoned even if your Parent says "But that's respectable work that will earn you a lot of money." Your Child may eagerly propose that you become an actor or actress. If, however, your Adult knows that you are unable to adapt to situations that involve competition and rejection, you may need to abandon that goal. If, in this case, your OK Critical Parent tells you "Very few people make a living as actors or actresses; why embark on a vagabond existence when you ought to be thinking about settling down?" and your Little Professor adds that "After you get settled, you can always join the community theatre and pursue acting as your hobby," then you've got two out of three votes against an acting career, and you had better look elsewhere. Your Little Professor did, however, manage to find a way to satisfy your "star-struck" needs.

If your Parent proposes that you go into your family business because it's safe and your Adult objects on the grounds that your talents require a different type of involvement, then it's important not to allow guilt feelings from your Child to manipulate you into upholding the family tradition. Checking out your Parent, Adult, and Child is how you reason things through, but keep in mind that your Little Professor may manipulate you into something that's totally impractical for you, your Natural Child may refuse to negotiate with your Adult and Parent, and your Adaptive Child may grab on to anything out of fear of failure or fear of hurting someone else. Your Adult may be so reasonable and rational that you end up compromising your feelings and your Parent so powerful and convincing that there is no room for what you want.

Remember that you can learn from every experience. Even though your first career choice may be Parent, Child, or Adult dominant, experience it, evaluate it, and then decide whether to stay with it. Based on your experience, your new decision will probably be better. Making your decision with a balanced ego-state portrait, however, will increase the chances that your new decision will indeed be better. Since you are living in a constantly changing and unpredictable world, you may find one day that you have outgrown the choice that was made with a balanced ego-state portrait. What is really right for you in your teens may not make you happy in your 20s, 30s, 50s, or 60s. The world of work may hold more excitement and promise for you if you view it as moving and growing rather than stagnant and yourself as able to grow with it.

Your next question may be "If I make my career-related decisions with a balanced ego-state portrait and therefore know that they are good for me, what about the people in my life I'm obligated to? What happens if what I want is incompatible with what my spouse, parents, fiancé, or children expect?" Some people hurt because they are doing what they want to be doing in life, and others hurt because they're not doing what they want to be doing in life. In establishing what you want out of life, it may be necessary to hurt or disappoint someone else rather than yourself. Disappointing someone else isn't easy, especially if that someone is an important person in your life.

If what you want and need for yourself is incompatible with what someone else has in mind for you, then it may be difficult for you to express your wants and needs to that person. It's sometimes easier to remain undecided or to do what someone else wants you to do. The fear of disappointing someone else and possibly losing his or her faith in you is sometimes enough to curb your desire to become who you want to become. The alternative, of course, is to disappoint and hurt yourself.

The goal is not to abandon the goals you have established for yourself but rather to learn how to use that same balanced portrait to negotiate your career plans with the important people in your life. (Transactions using a balanced portrait will be discussed in Chapter 19.)

In addition to using your balanced portrait to establish your career goals and discussing them with others, you can also use that portrait in getting and keeping your job. Regardless of how many years we spend training and preparing for our chosen vocation, we usually don't find ourselves automatically stepping into a job. We first encounter the standard prerequisite—namely, the interview. Many talented and highly skilled individuals have not gotten the jobs they wanted because they "flunked" their interviews. How, then, can we increase the chances of having a successful interview? If you take a balanced ego-state portrait into the interview with you, you are ready to analyze the transactions that will occur, and you will thus increase your chances of success.

Not only do you have to know how to "put your best foot forward" in an interview. In order to succeed on the job, you'll also have to continue to perform well. It's important that you be productive on the job, but you must also be compatible with people you work with. Most people spend a good portion of their lives at work, and therefore people who lack talent often are hired and remain on the job simply because they "fit in." If your ego-state portrait is balanced, you will be able to cope with most interpersonal situations that you confront on the job. This is not to say that you and the person you are dealing with will always part smiling, but at least you will know where you stand and others will know where they stand with you.

Exercise

 Stop and think about some of the jobs you've had, focusing in on two or three of them. If you have never had a job, think of a hobby, a volunteer job, school project, or committee work that you've done. Now draw the ego-state portrait you had in each of those jobs. What were your portraits like? Were they balanced? What does this tell you about yourself? Are you going to approach future jobs with a different portrait?

"What is my career-related attitude?" 15

Letting your VOCATIONAL POSITION
work for you

You can choose to place yourself in a superior (I'm OK, You're not-OK), inferior (I'm not-OK, You're OK), indifferent (I'm not-OK, You're not-OK), or equal (I'm OK, You're OK) position in your relationship with others. Your position or attitude may not affect whether you choose to become a doctor, dancer, teacher, executive, secretary, senator, fashion designer, lawyer, or housekeeper, but it will definitely affect how you operate within a given job. Feeling inferior to others doesn't mean that you won't become president of a company, but your attitude will determine how you treat your staff. Ideally, the president of the company and his or her staff would approach one another with an I'm OK, You're OK attitude, thus interacting with mutual or "equal" respect. In addition, your position determines how you approach your job. Let's look at how your vocational position may affect you and others and how you deal with your responsibilities in the world of work.

The Equal Position

The I'm OK, You're OK attitude toward your job and fellow workers is the most compatible position you can be in. A positive attitude allows you to approach any given situation with an open and accepting mind. *Unconditional love* is not a concept that should be reserved exclusively for your private life; it is appropriate in any situation that involves interactions with others. The I'm OK, You're OK position allows for the kind of unconditional fellowship that promotes the "team" approach to tackling work-related concerns. The focus is not on "Who

121

is going to outdo me?" or "Whom can I outdo?" but rather on "How can *we* resolve the issue at hand?"

Having an I'm OK, You're OK position doesn't mean that you're also functioning with a balanced ego-state portrait. For example, you may feel OK about yourself and most of the people at work, but your contaminated Adult may be discriminating unfairly against certain individuals in your work environment. Your Natural Child may exaggerate what OK means, and your Parent may smother everyone with nurturance. It is, therefore, important to approach your work situation not only with the I'm OK, You're OK position that promotes trust, understanding, and compatibility but also with a balanced ego-state portrait.

The Inferior Position

With the I'm not-OK, You're OK attitude you place yourself in an inferior or insecure position. More than likely you're the kind of person who seeks safety, and you will probably therefore look for safe, low-key jobs. You will select work that you can handle easily and that doesn't require much responsibility or important decision making. Even if you become an administrator or manager, you will probably rely on others to make your decisions for you. You may be easily swayed even from decisions that you have consulted many other people about. Such behavior leads to frustration, low morale, and lack of trust.

It's difficult to work with wishy-washy or unreliable people. Even in jobs that require very little responsibility, such people can upset the total work environment, for every job is a part of the whole. Employers have been known to hire people because of their dependent qualities, in the hope of molding them into employees who fit in, don't hassle anyone, and don't get in the way. What employers don't anticipate is that dependence and insecurity sometimes result in irresponsible performance and attitude.

The dependent personality may understand—and have—what it takes to succeed in the world of work but may not trust himself or herself to do what needs to be done in order to succeed. In addition, the I'm not-OK, You're OK type will typically allow himself or herself to be the victim of superiors as well as of fellow employees.

Another attitude that the I'm not-OK, You're OK personality can adopt is that of rescuer. Taking good care of others and putting them first, or devoting the self to pleasing others and fulfilling their aspirations can be another way of saying: "I'm not good enough, but you are." "I may know what it takes to succeed, but I don't have what it takes so I'll help you get to the top."

The Indifferent Position

Feeling not-OK about yourself and others doesn't necessarily mean that you can't feel OK about your work. Chances are that you have come to the conclusion that: "You can't help me." "I can't help myself." "I can't help you." or "You don't want to help me anyway." You may therefore escape into a job that requires a minimum of interpersonal contact. You may find success and satisfaction while working with "things" such as computers, cars, chemicals, and flowers but not with people. It's important for the I'm not-OK, You're not-OK individual to find solace at least in his or her work; if an individual feels uncomfortable with people, he or she will go through a great deal of stress and depression in the attempt to work with them. Rather than go through the pain of sneaking in and out of your office to avoid talking with anyone and rather than hide out while you're at work, why not look for a low-stress situation that requires very little interpersonal contact?

The Superior Position

If you don't trust anyone but yourself and if you believe your way of thinking and doing things is the only way, then you have assumed a very lonely position. People readily pick up "I'm better than you are" messages and will therefore more than likely stay out of your way. If you're in a leadership position, your condescending attitude will probably require that those who work for you revere you. You may be labeled "tyrant" or "dictator," and you may even like the image of ruling with an iron fist, but chances are that creativity in your work environment will be low. Others will be reluctant to approach you with a new idea if they know that you're the only one who can have new ideas. If you send messages that say "I don't need you," "You're in the way," "I can do it better myself," and "I have to put up with you," then your employees will respond with "I'm not needed, but I need the job." "I'm in the way, but I have to stay here because I can't find another job." "I can't do things as well as my boss can; as a matter of fact I always feel like I'm doing things the wrong way," "My boss is just putting up with me and will replace me the first chance she gets." The I'm OK, You're not-OK boss may like to hire the I'm not-OK, You're OK people who are easily controlled.

Those I'm OK, You're not-OK individuals who hold down lower-level jobs also communicate these "I don't need you" or "Stay away from me" messages. When individuals have convinced others that their advice and guidance is unwanted, then they're on their own. Being "on your own" is limiting in that you have only one source of input. Putting yourself in a superior or defensive position will make you incompatible with others. Your attitude closes doors between you and those you work with. Team work and cooperation are not a part of your frame of reference. Rather than treating others with respect and equality, you more than likely see yourself as giving others the "opportunity" to compromise themselves for you.

The I'm OK, You're not-OK type may not only select to feel superior to others in a defensive manner but also may choose to be a persecutor of people. When this is the case, it's almost impossible to do anything that meets with this person's approval, for he or she will "dig deep" to find excuses to punish others.

Exercises

Class Activity

As a group make a list of adjectives describing people who have adopted each of the four possible vocational positions. For example:

I'm not-OK, You're OK
is dependent
may be eager to please
may be scared
may feel helpless
may be a martyr
always puts self last

I'm not-OK, You're not-OK
is indifferent
doesn't like people
actively avoids people
wants a job that doesn't
    require people contact

I'm OK, You're not-OK
feels everyone is in need
    of help
likes to see people
    dependent

I'm OK, You're OK
is reliable
is flexible
is patient
is helpful
is respectable

Class Activity

Look at each of the positions described above and discuss in greater detail how an individual in each of the four vocational positions would operate in a given job. Discuss how likely it will be for each personality type to find success or happiness on the job and why you feel that to be the case.

Individual Activity

Think about your own vocational position. What has been your general vocational position in the jobs you've had? Are you going to continue operating with that attitude, or would you like to adopt a new position? Which one? Why?

Letting your VOCATIONAL SCRIPT work for you

Your attitude, or life position, may not determine what you do for a living, but your life script does do just that. If your life script describes you as impatient and pessimistic, it's not very likely that you'll fit into a job requiring that you wait for results and remain optimistic. You may also not fit into a slow and systematic promotion or salary-increase situation. If you've always been very overweight, then it's not likely that you'll become a model or athlete. If you have habitually traveled, then you probably won't be satisfied in a job that requires that you stay put. If you are accustomed to having money, you will more than likely not be happy with a low-paying job.

You may be saying "But there are plenty of people who grew up with a lot of money who hold down low-paying positions" and "I personally know a woman who was really fat growing up and turned out to be a model." People's life scripts do change, either because they want to change them or because the world around them requires that they change. To decide that, since you've always been rich, you would like to experience a middle-class life-style or, since you've always been fat, you now want to be a model demonstrates the power you can have over your life. In many situations, however, it's not you alone but the circumstances around you that shape your decision. The rich person may run out of money or have parents who refuse to share their money once their child becomes employable. Such circumstances require that a life script be changed or altered. The fat person may have found acceptance at home that made it comfortable for him or her to remain fat, but, after growing up and entering a social scene that rejected fatness, he or she changed the script in order to find acceptance.

Even though you can change or alter your life script at will, most people don't even think about doing so until they're confronted with such situations as divorce, marriage, loss of a job, physical or mental illness (their own or in the family), and economic depression (personal or nationwide).

You may feel that, if the world around you doesn't change drastically, you can at least identify the careers that would best suit the kind of person you are. In addition, you may have a pretty good idea of what you want your career to do for you and thus narrow your options down. You may want an opulent life-style, with a fancy home, fancy cars, and trips abroad, or you may simply want a roof over your head, anything that resembles a car that can get you from A to B, and a tent to go camping in. These scripts are very different; they describe very different personalities and therefore very different ambitions and career choices. Chances are that, if a war doesn't break out, if your family doesn't lose the business you've planned to go into, if the career of your choice isn't flooded with qualified people, and if you don't lose your health, then your expectations will more than likely materialize. There is one more factor that must be considered. Many people develop two very different scripts: one that fits their private lives and another that fits their public image. If, while growing up, you have not had a job or have had little contact with paid or volunteer group or committee work, then you probably have only one active script, your life script. You may, however, due to parent messages, have developed an imaginary vocational or public-image script; that is, you may have created a picture in your mind of the kind of career you "should" want for yourself, whether or not you're "supposed to" succeed in that career, and how you "ought" to behave in order to achieve your goal.

If you have already experienced the world of work or other forms of group involvement, then you probably already have an active public image or vocational script. You already know how you interact with others, how you strive for status within a group, and how hard you're willing to work with, for, or against group goals and group members. You can, therefore, predict pretty well where you're going in your career.

Your life script and public image or vocational script may be similar, but they may also be quite dissimilar. Your scripts may predict success at home and failure at work or vice versa, a strong person and a leader on the job and a meek "yes" person with the family or vice versa, a kind and helpful person on the job and a strict disciplinarian with spouse and children or vice versa. It's as if the "real" self can only come out in the environment that the person believes is safe. Rather than living two separate scripts, it may be less taxing, less confusing, and less frustrating to combine a balanced ego-state portrait with the I'm OK, You're OK position, a combination that works in any and every situation.

You may choose (or circumstances may force you) to change your script(s). Scripts aren't easy to alter; changing habitual behavior patterns requires time and patience. Transition is tough, but it doesn't have to be out of control and haphazard. You can choose to gain power over yourself; that is, you can study your past and current behavior patterns and identify what you want to keep and what you want to discard. You can clearly paint a new picture, a new image of who you are and where you want to go.

Exercises

Individual Activity

Make a list of adjectives that describe you. The longer your list, the better you'll understand your script. Your list may look like this:

Adjectives that Describe Me

conscientious	studious	cooperative
highly motivated	responsible	happy
creative	attractive	leader type
ambitious	patient	versatile
carefree	sensitive	affectionate
success-oriented	flexible	gutsy

Make a list of what you want your career to do for you. You don't have to know exactly what your career will be in order to know what you want from it. Here is a sample list.

What I Want from My Career

money ($100,000 a year)	flexible work hours
fame	a chance to write
acceptance	opportunity to travel
recognition	national and
freedom	international
private plush office	friends

Make two lists, one that describes how you see yourself behaving in your private world and another that describes how you see yourself behaving in the world of work.

My Private-Life Script	*My Public-Image, Vocational Script*
spontaneous	more controlled
lazy	regulated
carefree	responsible most of the time
responsible when	compromising to a point
appropriate	patient
uncompromising	optimistic
patient	
optimistic	
single	

Class Activity

Look at the sample lists and study them. Now name some possible careers that the individual described by these lists could pursue. Discuss why you feel that this hypothetical individual should look toward the career(s) you suggest.

Individual Activity

Now go over your lists and identify some possible career choices for yourself.

Small-Group Activity

Discuss your career choices and explain why you feel that they would be "right" for you. Share your list with the other members of the group and see whether the group agrees with the qualities you have used to describe yourself and whether you have selected logical career options for yourself.

"How can I give and take in the world of work?" 17

"How can I give and take in the world of work?"

Letting your VOCATIONAL STROKES work for you

Recognition is a term that is used frequently in the world of work. People often bend over backwards to receive it, because in this world recognition is synonymous with salary increases and promotions. But before we even get to our first job, recognition or stroking has already shaped and molded our career-related decisions and attitudes. The recognition we received as children influenced our vocational scripting. For example, if we received positive stroking, or reinforcement, for what we dreamed about becoming, then the chances are that we remained in that track. If, however, we received negative stroking, such as ridicule, we may have changed to an occupational outlook that received positive reinforcement. Some of us may not have received positive stroking but were successful in getting attention by proposing unacceptable career choices. By stimulating unpleasant arguments from significant others and experiencing their manipulative tactics to get us to change our goals, we were negatively stroked—which was better than not being stroked at all.

This stroke-getting strategy, if it becomes habit, typically finds us fulfilling a vocational script that "they" opposed and that may also be far from what we really want for ourselves. It's unfortunate to adopt the attitude that "It doesn't matter what I do as long as it's not what 'they' want me to do." We do grow accustomed to a stroke-getting strategy, and we usually end up taking that strategy to work with us.

If your vocational script was shaped by your need for stroking, then your decision was externally controlled and didn't emerge from within you. Our stroke hunger is so great that stroking does become a powerful manipulator. Sometimes we become so wrapped up in trying to get our stroke needs met through others that we forget all about our

130

ability to meet many of our stroke needs ourselves. You have the power to stroke, reward, reinforce, and recognize yourself, and learning how to do that will provide you with much of the total satisfaction that you need. You have the capacity to get to know yourself better than anyone else possibly can. It's therefore logical to assume that, if you take the time to learn about yourself, you will find out how to do what's best for you and you will learn what makes you feel good about yourself. Once you know what makes you feel good about yourself, you can move in that direction and experience satisfaction. Such satisfaction is addictive and becomes the self-motivator or self-reward system you need in order to meet your responsibilities. As you become less dependent on others for your stroke needs, you will find yourself more in control of yourself and less likely to be manipulated by the people you work with.

The idea is not to exclude our need for external stimulation, because that's impossible to do. Rather, the goal is to become more internally controlled, allowing more of our motivation to come from within ourselves. You can make sure that the stroking that comes from within you is positive and not negative, but you don't have that kind of control over your external sources. You will need your positive stroking to help yourself get started in the career you want and to successfully maintain it. Just as you can use your OK Critical Parent to warn yourself about laziness and procrastination, you can use your Nurturing Parent to pat yourself on the back, pick yourself up when you're down, and put yourself back on the right track again. You can be tolerant and self-accepting, which are important qualities to have when goals need to be clarified and deadlines need to be met.

Another excellent source of positive stroking is your Adult computer. Rather than storing negative data, you can sift and sort through incoming data, weigh them carefully, and concentrate on storing "success" experiences and strategies that can help you get and keep the job you want. By dwelling on the "good," you can automatically stroke yourself into a "Yes, I can" attitude, which is the prerequisite to establishing desirable goals, reaching them, and experiencing them with pleasure.

Your Natural Child can help you by giving you the ability to express how you feel. Giving yourself permission to level with your family, and later with those you work with, about your career goals in an honest and open manner is indeed self-rewarding and energizing. Don't forget to use your Adult's reasoning power and your OK Critical Parent's judgment to temper your Natural Child. In addition, your Natural Child is great at sizing things up clearly, which is a "plus" on the job. Your Adaptive Child will improve your judgment, because it is tuned into what's expected of you and is willing to accommodate the self. Your Adult and OK Parent know how to balance that Child so that you will do this appropriately. Being able to coordinate yourself is a self-reassuring form of positive stroking. Your cunning and creative Little Professor will help you the most in learning about the "good" you have inside you and in using that to your best advantage.

Life is unpredictable. Since you are the recipient of what you allow to affect you and of what you do to and for yourself, why not learn to filter out the negative and allow the positive strokes to run your life? Such a habit may reduce your apprehension about the future; once you know that you will be giving yourself positive strokes, then you can feel secure that, no matter what the future holds, you'll be making the best and the most of every situation you encounter. Such conscientious self-care leads to a positive self-image and a positive outlook in your world of work.

Another strategy that will help you accentuate the positive is not only rewarding yourself for the positive things you do but also rewarding others whenever they do something you like. Every positive act should be recognized. If you do something good for yourself, think about it. Pay attention to how good that really feels. Savor it, wallow in it, and possess it. If someone else does something that makes you feel good about yourself, let them know it. You can do this both verbally and nonverbally. You have the power to become the positive person you want to be, and you can also reinforce others to treat you in a positive manner. On the job, you don't have to spend a lot of time thinking about how others behave toward you; simply notice when they do something nice for you or are treating you well and show them that you appreciate it.

Dwelling on "Poor me, I can't seem to do anything right. I'm going to disappoint my boss again" can be gratifying. People often derive pleasure from wallowing in self-pity. Putting yourself down can become a habit you can't do without. Such negative self-stroking often results in a negative self-image that tells you not to try to help yourself because you're hopeless. Once you believe you're hopeless, it's not very likely that you'll care about what happens to you or take the trouble to identify the "good" within yourself and start building on that.

People are walking, talking collections of positive and negative life experiences, some of which they did have control over and others of which they couldn't or wouldn't control. The one thing everyone does have control over is what he or she chooses to spend time thinking about and feeling. The pessimist dwells on the negative and foresees negative outcomes; the optimist dwells on the positive and sees positive outcomes. Pessimists stroke themselves conditionally; that is, they choose to perceive themselves as the victims of social conditions and typically occupy themselves with wishing that they could have handled these conditions differently than they did. The optimist, on the other hand, expects to "blow it" now and then and expects to be faced with challenging conditions but doesn't spend much time kicking himself or herself. Instead, the optimist accepts the self unconditionally; that is, he or she likes the self and sees the self as OK. The conditions are simply the natural ups and downs that one expects to cope with.

Exercise

The following exercise is designed to help you develop your positive-stroke potential.

Individual Activity

Take the time to focus on what you've done and experienced today. Now make a list of all the positive strokes you gave yourself and all the positive strokes you received from others. In other words, what happened today that made you feel good?

If you can't list many or any, don't worry. You can increase the positive strokes you give yourself, and you can even do something about increasing the positive strokes you receive from others. You do have to pace yourself and accomplish this a little at a time, one day at a time.

By keeping up with your lists on a daily basis you will actually train yourself to focus on the positive things that happen to you. You will become more aware of how you allow yourself and others to be negative with you, and you will therefore know what you want to decrease or eliminate.

Letting your *TIME STRUCTURING* *work for you*

Before you select a career for yourself, you need to clarify how you want that career to structure your time on and off the job. Statistics generally indicate that only 15% of people who are gainfully employed are happy with their work; therefore it appears that 85% of those who are working find their careers undesirable for one reason or another. How you feel about your job affects your personal life. We can, therefore, conclude that a tremendous number of people are unhappy both at work and at home. Unhappy people typically structure their time to avoid the undesirable. Although they may be physically present, they will nevertheless engage in escape strategies, such as withdrawals, activities, rituals, and pastimes, to relieve boredom, frustration, disappointment, and their anger about sacrificing precious time in unsatisfying situations. It is therefore important that, before you select your career, you think about such questions as:

"Do I want an 8-to-5 job?"
"Do I want to be able to establish my own work schedule?"
"Do I want to spend my time working with people?"
"Do I want to spend my time creating with my hands?"
"Do I want to spend my time thinking up ideas?"
"Do I want to work nights?"
"Do I want to clock in and clock out?"

Once you start working, you'll be concerned with other questions, such as:

134

"Do I want to work overtime to get this done?"
"Can I afford the time to go to lunch with a friend?"
"Since I have to be at work at 8 in the morning, should I go out tonight?"
"Do I have time for a coffee break?"
"Should I go out of town to a conference, or should I stay here and finish the report for my boss?"

It may be helpful to you to become aware of how people who are dissatisfied with their work situation employ avoidance strategies. These strategies are common because they're easy to use—so easy, in fact, that most people don't even know they're using them. If you're bored, angry, or frustrated with a situation and if there seems to be no solution to the problem, then you will consciously or unconsciously employ withdrawals, rituals, pastimes, activities, and games. People do quit when they've had enough, but usually they don't simply walk out of an undesirable work situation. They stay until they find an acceptable alternative. If an alternative does not materialize for a long time, people often resign themselves to their situations, saying: "Well, that's the way things are." "Who said life was supposed to be easy." "I don't know anyone who is enjoying his or her work, and why should I be any different?" And so they sink deeper and deeper into their undesirable work situation until they become apathetic and numb. They may even stop searching for alternatives.

Withdrawals

Most of us have been taught to think before we act. We may, therefore, find ourselves thinking and thinking without ever once thinking that it's time to act. You may start out by trying to come up with solutions to an undesirable job situation, but the longer you postpone action, the more and more difficult it may become to do anything about helping yourself. We may learn first to withdraw into our minds to think of solutions; soon we find ourselves fantasizing or daydreaming without ever getting to the stage of trying out something new or making a commitment to actively pursue a new direction.

People who use withdrawal tactics frequently come across to others as preoccupied, unaware of what's going on around them, and indifferent to people, their responsibilities, and themselves.

Activities

A popular avoidance strategy that becomes very powerful when combined with withdrawals is preoccupation with activities. Keeping busy with endless meetings, conferences, and telephone calls may allow you to appear productive; you may even think you're accomplishing something, when in fact you are merely "killing time." You may frequently hear yourself saying "I've got so much to do," "I'm always swamped," "I never have time to stop and think." You may actually become too busy to address important job-related issues.

Rituals

Ritualistic thinking and behavior patterns are a part of every established work environment. Whom you go to lunch with, where you eat, where and when and with whom you have your coffee breaks, where you park your car, when you're expected to arrive and leave work, whom you may or may not address directly in the hierarchy, what you wear, and how much vacation time you have are the kinds of rituals that regulate the world of work.

There are other traditions that regulate that world, such as stereotypical ideas about responsibilities and behavior and feeling patterns that are expected from a man, a woman, a Black, a new employee, a Jew, a college graduate, the son of the boss, and the boss. Ritualistic thinking patterns are difficult to challenge. New ideas that might be excellent for a company are often rejected if "That's not the way we do things around here." Rituals, whether they're old fashioned, modern, or somewhere in between, will continue to remain a part of all establishments. Because that's exactly what the "establishment" is—an established way of doing things. Rituals are therefore reality, an expected and, we hope respected, way of doing things. But, if rituals become not-OK and begin to interfere with growth and interpersonal compatibility, then they need to be reexamined.

Pastimes

Safe talk about the weather, what you did on the weekend, and what you're going to have for dinner is a pleasant way to pass the time during coffee breaks or when you happen to run into a fellow employee. It's a good way to momentarily get your mind off what you're working on. If pastimes, however, predominate your time on the job—that is, if you're constantly seeking out people to chat with or if you get many personal phone calls at work—then you may be employing pastimes as an escape strategy. If you look closely, you may even find that, in important meetings or other situations in which you should be concerned with work-related projects and issues, you pass the time in meaningless conversation that sounds good but goes nowhere.

Games

When you stay at the same job with the same people for a long time, you will probably be or will want to appear to be more involved with that environment. This is when games that resemble open and honest commitment may be adopted as your interpersonal coping strategy. We discussed games thoroughly in Chapter 8. Go back and reacquaint yourself with the games people play, and then do the following:

1. As you read about each game, think about its role in the world of work.
2. Think about how you may be playing these games and how they affect your relationships at work and in other group situations.
3. Think about how these games may have affected or will affect how you fulfill your work-related responsibilities.
4. Think about the people you've been close to or have been assigned to work with closely; identify the games they play.
5. How did the games your fellow employees or group members played affect you, and how did you react to these games?

Whenever you find yourself constantly avoiding any situation —something you're faced with at work or elsewhere—then it's appropriate to ask yourself: "What am I avoiding?" and "Why am I avoiding?" The desire to escape comes not only from having selected the wrong career or the wrong job situation but also from being afraid of failure or rejection or from not feeling properly prepared for the work you're doing or are about to do. In order to find intimacy at work with your fellow employees and in order to keep withdrawals, activities, rituals, pastimes, and games at a reasonable level, you must be thoroughly familiar with what you're getting into and feel prepared to meet the challenges of your work.

Exercise

    As a class, share the experiences you have had—on the job or in school, committee, or other volunteer-group involvements —that were related to avoidance strategies. You can probably identify (don't mention names) individuals who mastered specific strategies or combinations of these escape tactics. Discuss what they did and how that made you feel. Were you glad to engage in withdrawals, pastimes, rituals, activities, and/or games with them, or were you annoyed? Also think about how and why you engaged in these tactics and how that makes you feel right now. Share your thoughts and feelings with the group if you like.

Letting your VOCATIONAL

TRANSACTIONS

work for you

Communication is the sum total of how we stroke and how we structure time. Although much of what we think and feel is exchanged via nonverbal behavior, most of our actions are accompanied by verbal messages. Have you thought about the fact that we typically formulate a physical expression in order to prepare others for what we're about to say? We tend to set the mood nonverbally, and, if we're tuned into each other, we can almost predict what is going to be said. Although it's often true that "actions speak louder than words," we typically focus on what is verbalized, take that at face value, and consider nonverbal messages as an afterthought. It may be helpful to focus on the nonverbal when you're analyzing the verbal transactions. If what someone said puzzles you, analyzing the verbal transactions alone may not help you explain what happened. If you think through the nonverbal transactions and the messages they communicated, you may be able to clarify what happened.

Becoming skillful with both verbal and nonverbal transactional analysis will help you figure out what's going on between you and others at work; it will also help you prepare for such situations as interviews and conferences with your boss or other important people in your life. Once you get to know people, you can often predict how they are going to react to certain situations; in other words, you acquire a feel for their life script and vocational script. When you analyze the transactions between you and another person, you may not know immediately what happened. But when you figure it out, you probably won't feel surprised that it happened. If, in fact, you know the people you're with well enough to predict what they're going to say and do, then you can restructure how you transact with them in order to change how they respond to you.

At work you can stop punishing people for what they don't do and start rewarding them for what they do. Instead of focusing in on undesirable behavior, you can ignore it and thus work toward extinguishing it. As you will recall, we have already mentioned that punishments and rewards are both strong reinforcers and that ignoring something you don't like will extinguish it.

It's easier to analyze transactions and to understand what's going on when you know someone well. Many life situations, however, such as job interviews, require that you come face-to-face with a total stranger and analyze what is going on between the two of you moment by moment. This is when a balanced ego-state portrait and an I'm OK, You're OK position really come in handy. If you take a balanced portrait and a positive position into your interview, you won't be defensive or have preconceived notions of what's about to happen. Thus you can leave yourself open to alert analysis of the transactions that are about to occur.

Each person you're about to meet for the first time approaches you with his or her own ego-state portrait and position, which interact with your portrait and position. Since you're meeting for the first time, you have no way of knowing that interviewer's script and will therefore not be able to predict his or her behavior, but your ability to analyze transactions on the spot will increase your chances to succeed.

When you meet an interviewer, be aware of which ego state he or she is in. You may be greeted by an OK Critical, not-OK Critical, or Nurturant Parent; you may be greeted by a computer-like individual or one who is contaminated with prejudice or fantasy; you may be greeted by a Natural or Adaptive Child or a Little Professor; or you may encounter a balanced ego-state portrait. Regardless of which personality type you encounter, your success will hinge on how you use your ego-state portrait to transact with your interviewer. If your attitude is I'm OK, You're OK, then you can cope regardless of which position your interviewer is in. If your interviewer is coming from the not-OK Critical Parent and the I'm OK, You're not-OK position just because you're a woman interviewing for what he or she considers a man's job, you may tend to respond with your apologetic and inferior Adaptive Child or an equally not-OK Critical Parent that retaliates with hostility and anger. Instead, however, you might use your ego-state portrait as follows:

(1) your Adaptive Child can be respectful;
(2) your Natural Child can express your feelings;
(3) your OK Critical Parent's wisdom can temper those feelings so that they come across as nonpunitive;
(4) your Little Professor's alertness can detect game playing;
(5) your Adult can talk about your skills and talents; and, again,
(6) your Little Professor can explain how your skills are unique and how you can fill the job better than anyone else.

Even if you don't get the job, you'll walk away knowing that you handled a tough situation well.

You may also find yourself in a situation that calls for confronting your parents or other important people in your life with your career choice. If what you want isn't what they want for you and if you're used to giving in to them and would like to change that, then it's time to unscramble what's happening when you transact with them. Since they are important to you, you are probably familiar with their scripts and able to predict what will probably take place in your encounter. You can then use your Adult to reconstruct your transactions with them and plan to use a balanced portrait and an I'm OK, You're OK position to change your communication patterns. In order to alter your transactions, you need to ask yourself such questions as: "What do they say and do to change my mind about what I want?" "What can I say and do in order to stick to what I want?"

The seven-step action plan in Chapter 20 deals with this situation specifically. But before you turn to that chapter, figure out a course of action you might undertake. Then compare that with what the plan suggests. Closely scrutinize what's going on in your current transactions, and decide how you would like to change them. First, diagram a specific set of transactions as they typically occur, and then diagram them the way you would like them to occur. Chapter 9 will refresh your ability to diagram and analyze transactions. Don't forget to look for ulterior motives, the hidden persuaders or manipulaters that may be influencing you indirectly. Whenever you've had a "good" talk with someone but find yourself fighting doubts and discomfort that you can't account for, reconstruct the transactions and look for ulterior motives.

In addition to diagraming and analyzing transactions, another good strategy is to observe others while they role play specific situations. Watching your classmates or friends act out an encounter that you have experienced or fear experiencing will help you become aware of how you actually communicate with the important people in your life and why your transactions work the way they do. Better communication skills are not a guarantee against hurt and disappointment. Skillful transactions, however, can help you achieve your goals with less confusion for all concerned.

Exercises

 Take turns role playing different situations for one another; then, in small groups (three or four people each), discuss how the transactions could be altered in order to break down communication barriers and increase the chances of achieving your desired goal.

These role-play situations may reflect real concerns that members of your class are trying to cope with, or they may be hypothetical. The following are suggested situations you may want to start with, but real concerns or hypothetical concerns suggested by group members will be the most helpful situations to deal with. The group members' suggestions will always be more timely, relevant, and typical of the group members involved. Use your small groups as a support system to help you work through personal situations.

1. A father is doing his best to convince his son, who wants to become an artist, to go to law school.
2. A mother and father are trying to convince their daughter, who has decided to go to medical school, that she shouldn't waste her time and their money because she'll end up getting married and raising a family anyway.
3. The daughter wants to get married, and her parents want her to go to college.
4. A husband is trying to convince his wife not to go back to school to become a nurse, and she's determined to do just that.
5. A father tells his son that he will buy him a new car if he decides to go to college. The son doesn't want to go to college. He wants to become a mechanic because he loves to work on cars.
6. You are talking with your boss about a raise.

7. You are telling a parent or relative that you need more money to stay in school.
8. A woman is trying to convince her fiancé that they should get married and that she will support him through school.
9. An employee is confronting the boss about free time to get additional training.
10. A husband is telling his wife that he is going to change his career and life-style and letting her know that he would like her to be a part of his new life.
11. A wife is telling her husband that she wants a career of her own and that she wants him to share household duties and concerns equally with her.

Letting the SEVEN-STEP ACTION PLAN *work for you*

You have learned how to apply the seven-step action plan to your personal concerns. Now let's practice applying it to specific career-related situations. You can use it to help clarify your goals, to establish better communication channels with others, and to improve your decision making. If you want to cope in a well-organized and systematic manner, this action plan can help you learn to do so.

Again, let's follow this action plan step by step. The career-related example we will use to demonstrate how to apply the plan is: "How do I tell my parents that I'm not going to major in political science and then go on to law school and that I plan to become an artist instead?"

1. Identify Your Goal

The goal clarified in TA terms is: "How do I utilize a *balanced ego-state portrait* and an *I'm OK, You're OK position* to *transact* to my parents, via *positive* and *unconditional strokes* and wise utilization of time, the *vocational script* that *I* want to follow?"

Here again it may be appropriate for you to list all your career-related concerns and then select the one that attracts you the most to work on.

2. Understand Your Goal

What's the current undesirable situation between me and my parents?
1. We're avoiding each other because we know that we have

   things to discuss that none of us wants to hear.
2. Every time we do have a conversation we end up arguing about law school. It's always the same.
3. They can't seem to understand that I don't want to go to law school.
4. They believe that I don't know what I want to do anyway, so I should at least get started in that direction. (I know now, but I didn't for a long time.)
5. Now that I know I want to go to art school, I'm reluctant to tell them because I'm afraid of hurting their feelings.
6. I'm also afraid that they will refuse to "foot the bill" and that I'll have to work my way through school.

What's motivating me to deal with this problem now?
1. I feel that I have a right to set my own career goals.
2. I'm aware of the fact that what I do vocationally will influence other aspects of how I live my life.
3. I realize how important it is to be in control of my own destiny.
4. I've been putting things off for too long, and it's time to decide what school I'm going to attend.
5. I want my parents to understand that I have a right to explore and experiment with the path I want to travel in life.
6. I'm ready to accept the responsibility of working my way through school if I need to.

What am I going to gain by reaching this goal?
1. I will feel self-respect.
2. I will be able to do what I want to do.
3. I will be establishing myself as an individual, making my own decisions.
4. I will open up new communication channels between me and my parents.
5. I will find out whether I can actually sit down with my parents and actively, systematically, and respectfully help them to understand that I have to lead my own life now.
6. If we reach a clear understanding of where we stand and can respect each other's position, they may feel that they can support me financially and emotionally in my endeavor.

Now answer these same questions about your own goal.

3. Take Full
Responsibility for Reaching Your Goal

How do I feel about this goal? Am I giving myself permission to see this through? Have I analyzed the traditional script and the transactions that always result in argument and new avoidance tactics? Have I looked at how I can approach the situation from an I'm OK, You're OK position and with a balanced ego-state portrait? Have I checked the situation out with an individual or individuals I trust in order to get feedback and more ideas? Would it be helpful to get a support group together that could help me (and them) work through this situation?

4. Describe
Your Action Plan and Set Time Limits

I know what my goal is, I want to reach it, and these are the steps I'm going to take to initiate action. Once I complete this plan I will reassess the situation and continue with a plan that will logically build on the initial plan. I will continue to do this until I reach my goal.

What am I going to do to start working on my goal?
1. I am going to set a time when my parents and I can sit down and talk for at least two hours. I'll ask them for an entire evening just in case it takes that long.
2. I am going to explain to them that I want to go to art school and that I want to become an artist for the following reasons:
   a. I have talent in that area.
   b. I get a great deal of pleasure from expressing myself through my art.
   c. I like the life-style that artists lead, and I have researched the kinds of opportunities I will have in the world of work once I finish school. (I will explain this thoroughly to my parents.)
   d. I want to be happy in life, and, even though the world of art may prove to be wrong for me in the long run, I owe it to myself at least to give it a chance. Yes, I may turn out to be a "starving artist," but that's the chance I want to take.
3. I will be kind and respectful of my parents' feelings, because I do love them; I don't have to hurt them or put them down

in order to live my own life.

4. I will be open to further discussions. A decision doesn't have to be made right away about how they see their role in my endeavor. I'll give them time to absorb what I've said and to think things through.

When am I going to start and when am I going to finish working on my goal?

I will initiate this plan when we first sit down to talk about my career goals (a week from Friday). During our first session I will request that we set aside time once a week to discuss this and related matters further. I want to make ·re that everything each of us needs and wants to say gets saiu. This often takes time. People often aren't in touch with their innermost feelings, and, even when they are, it takes time for them to feel comfortable enough to express them. After we get started with these weekly discussions, they may turn out to be something the three of us want to adopt on a weekly basis to work on family concerns. During our second or third session I will recommend that we continue meeting weekly.

Now it's your turn to sit down and figure out when you're going to start and when you're going to finish.

5. Establish a Stroke System to Help You Reach Your Goal

The stroke system in this example could be the support group. The group could establish weekly or semi-monthly meeting times to discuss progress and new points of view of each situation. In addition, each member of the support group could select one individual in that group to talk with privately as needed. If the support group shares a common concern, then more in-depth understanding and ideas will be generated for each of the members. The support group should probably consist of no more than four individuals.

6. Clarify How You and Others Will Know that Your Goal Has Been Reached

I understand that I may not succeed. My parents may not be receptive to my ideas. I will, however, give it all I've got, and I will discuss each situation with my support group. Not only will I give all of my ideas a chance, but I will also try out my support group's suggestions.

> *I will know that I have reached my goal when:*
> 1. I have clearly told my parents where I stand and what my plans are.
> 2. I actually hear them saying "We understand why you want to become an artist. Even though we feel you're making a mistake, we also see that you have your mind made up, and we therefore have no choice but to let you do what you want with your life."
> 3. I have been accepted into an art school.
> 4. I announce to my parents that I have been accepted to an art school.
> 5. I find that, whether or not we see eye-to-eye, we're still trying to work things out in our weekly sessions.
> 6. I am feeling good about starting art school even if my parents are still rejecting my plans.

Now list how you will know that you have reached your goal.

> *I will know that my parents know a change has taken place when:*
> 1. I'm comfortable with myself and have been fair with them.
> 2. they stop resisting me with all the reasons why I should do what they want and acknowledge my career choice.
> 3. they are willing to give my idea a chance.
> 4. we don't end our discussions with disagreement, anger, and new avoidance strategies.
> 5. they ask questions about art school and show genuine interest in hearing about my school plans and what I plan to do with my degree.

It's your turn again to list how you will know that "they" know a change has taken place.

7. Write a Contract with Yourself

Using the same format you used in Chapter 10, make a contract with yourself to achieve your desired goal.

Conclusion

"Where Am I Going?" In this section of the book you have had the opportunity to ask yourself that question and to thoroughly explore it. Taking yourself where you want to go in life requires that you view life as flexible; the road not taken at one point may be the right route to travel at another point in time. You can opt to be career "wise" or foolish. You can choose to express your individuality and identity through your career, or you can choose to ignore your feelings in favor of what others want from you. You may already know what you want to do, or you may not. Regardless of whether or not you've finalized your occupational choice, you will still need to research thoroughly and, if possible, try out your goal before you devote your full-time energy to it.

In order to get where you're going, you need to trust yourself and selected others who can enrich you with information or ideas you hadn't thought of before. The goal, of course, is not to become reliant on external controls but to use friends, relatives, books, magazines, and people employed in the field to enrich your data base. A solid data base will enable you to arrive at decisions that come from within you. The goal is to achieve self-motivation and increased internal control and not to allow a lack of information and self-trust to force you into accepting the controls of others.

Talking with other people and negotiating with them about occupational outlooks and your occupational desires is important, for your career decisions will, in fact, influence the people you will be associating with or living with while employed in that field. Being courteous and considerate of others doesn't require that you give up your goal; all it requires is that you help them understand where you're going and why you've selected that goal for yourself.

Section III

HOW DO I GET THERE?

Setting a goal is one thing; reaching it is quite another, especially when that goal requires long-range planning. If we look at career goals, there are very few that don't require either a technical, a vocational, or a college background. This means that a training period of at least six months to perhaps ten years may stand between you and your career. Since an education or training period is typically required to get you where you're going, this section of the book will focus on how to make it through the school experience. It may take only six months to become a clerk-typist, but it may take ten years of college or even longer to acquire a Ph.D. Regardless of how long it takes, however, there is a period of adjustment for every individual who becomes a student.

The transition from homemaker, high school student, or working person to college student requires that you incorporate a totally new set of rules and responsibilities into your life. This isn't easy, and for some people it is even impossible. Students do drop out of school for many reasons, including being unable to cope with the new environment and not knowing how to integrate the status of student into established patterns of day-to-day living.

Becoming a student involves more than simply adjusting to school. It means integrating, as harmoniously as possible, the new world with the existing personal world, and for many people this existing world may include the world of work. Making each world an integral part of the other will help increase the chances for success in school, on the job, and at home. The goal is to maximize harmony. This is not to say that discord must be avoided at all cost; rather, the goal is to understand the dynamics involved in creating harmony so that we can maximize it when we want to.

The following are situations that often plague students:

1. How do I cope with the grievances of my neglected spouse? They may sound like this: "All you ever do is study. We never have fun any more." "If I'm going to support you through school, you'd better not take me for granted."
2. How do I cope with family demands such as: "Thanksgiving is a family tradition, and, exams or not, we expect you to be here." Or "We're paying for an education, not for a vacation."
3. How do I cope with "Odd Couple" roommate problems such as: "What do you mean, you're 'having a few friends drop in tonight'? I've got an exam in the morning!"
4. How do I learn to discipline myself so that I can behave differently than: "Oh, well, so I flunk another exam. Let's start the party!"
5. How can I help my children understand that spending less time with them doesn't mean that I love them less?
6. How can I cope with professors or employers who are not as understanding as I hoped they would be and who confront me with: "I'm not interested in your problems. A due date is a due date, and I expect you to complete your work on time."

Students seldom have difficulty recognizing that things could be better, but understanding how to successfully cope with such problems may be difficult or impossible. Consequently, typical problem-solving strategies may go something like this:

> "No one understands me."
> "When I keep up with my school work, my boss and family get on my back."
> "When I do my best to keep my job, school and my personal life suffer."
> "When I attend to my personal world—you've guessed it—my school work and my on-the-job performance fall flat."
> "I can't take it anymore. I quit."

When the student gets to this point, a new question arises: "What should I quit? Should I give up my job, school, or the person I'm living with?" The student can learn how to successfully solve these problems before they get out of hand, but if he or she lacks the skills to cope with such experiences, helplessness, frustration, anger, or indifference may set in. These feelings often result in negative problem-solving strategies such as walking out, blaming others for one's own shortcomings, turning negative feelings inward to hurt oneself, or simply giving up and living in undesirable circumstances without trying to change things. At this point the obvious question is: "How does one adjust?" or "How does one integrate new aspects of living into established patterns and routines?" This section of the book will provide you with the opportunity to take a good look at what stepping into a new world—namely the student's world—is all about, how to cope in that new world, and how to integrate that world into established patterns of living so that your goals can be realized harmoniously and with pleasure.

"Who's controlling how I get there?" 21

Letting your *PARENT* educate you

Reaching long-range goals is a painful process; for many individuals it is impossible. The reason for this is obvious when Parent messages are examined. Some people plague and torture themselves with failure-oriented injunctions such as:

> "It takes a lot of money to get an education, and I can't afford it."
> "I'm a girl and am therefore not supposed to succeed."
> "I've always blown it in school, and I won't make it this time either."
> "I'm stuck in a wheelchair, and I don't want to go to school because I'll feel uncomfortable."

People who are failure oriented or have blocked their striving toward their educational goals simply because they're women or because they're physically or financially handicapped are excusing themselves from exploring the many opportunities and resources that are available to them.

Just as some people block themselves with failure messages, others fortify themselves with high-pressure "be perfect" messages that typically also ensure failure. Such messages include:

> "I have to be better than anyone else, or I won't make it."
> "I have to get all A's and I have to be liked by all of my professors, or I won't get the job I want."
> "I have to sacrifice everything and endure at all cost if I'm going to reach my goal."

155

Such "success at all cost" messages carry expensive price tags with them. Students who force themselves to continuously remain in high gear while chasing after that diploma or certificate may be endangering not only their emotional and physical health but also their interpersonal relationships.

There are few students who don't plague themselves with "fear of failure" and who don't make sacrifices in order to succeed in school, but such not-OK Critical Parent messages ensure failure. A spouse, a teacher, or an employer will ultimately give up on a failure-oriented person and allow him or her to go ahead and fail. Many people reach a point at which they can no longer endure the "success at all cost" kind of pressure and retreat to someone or something that involves less stress and self-compromise.

The failure-oriented person doesn't expect to succeed, and the "success at all cost" person doesn't expect to fail. The first type doesn't believe in internal satisfaction, and the second feels that gratification can occur only after that ultimate goal has been reached; in other words, he or she believes that it's worth sacrificing yourself for what's to come in the future and thus puts "living" life on hold. Both types set themselves up for continuous disappointment.

Students can and do confuse unreasonable Parent messages with being responsible. Being responsible is the key to success in school, but living up to the demands of your not-OK Critical Parent does not represent responsible behavior. Being too demanding or too hard on yourself or not demanding enough or not hard enough on yourself is just what it takes *not* to succeed. Students often give up, and others give up on them, because they get tired of their slow, low-energy pace that doesn't seem to bring them any closer to their goal or because they can't possibly live up to the unreasonable high-pressure tempo they've set in order to get there.

Student status may be temporary, but life, after all, is lived day-by-day and some people are not as tolerant as others. To some, sacrificing for six months or even ten years to reach a goal is acceptable. To others, six days may be six too many. Regardless of how long the student is willing to commit himself or herself to a goal, he or she cannot automatically assume that others will survive that time period with them. Others may try it, but they may not be able to do so in the long run, especially when that goal doesn't seem to get any closer or when the pace to get there becomes too unbearable.

Even if the student learns to minimize not-OK Critical Parent messages, he or she may find that that's not enough to ensure success.

Without replacing that not-OK Critical Parent with OK messages and without a Nurturing Parent to provide encouragement when the going gets tough, chances are that goal attainment may still be left to chance. Rather than allowing not-OK Critical Parent messages to dominate your performance as a student, perhaps you should learn to live with OK Critical Parent messages such as:

> "I should pace myself so that there is time to study, time for my job, time for those I care about, and time for myself."
> "I should plan to spend at least half an hour on weekdays really interacting with the person or people I am living with and more time on weekends."
> "I should plan an exercise program for myself and stick to it."
> "I should have realistic visions about how long it's going to take me to get my degree, for I must remember that I have responsibilities to my family, my boss, my friends, my health, and myself."
> "I should eat regularly even during high-pressure exam weeks."
> "I should let my friends know when I plan to study and tell them not to contact me during those hours."
> "I should check out whether or not I have deficiencies in math, reading, or English and plan to brush up on those skills."
> "I should be careful about how I spend my money, because I'm only working part-time and I'm used to a full-time salary."
> "I should stick to schedule and get my assignments in on time."

In addition to these OK Critical messages, you will find that knowing how to use your Nurturing Parent to help you through school is a skill you can't do without. Not only will you need to know how to comfort yourself when your school work doesn't meet with the kind of approval you expected, when everything starts to pile up and you just don't know how you're going to get it all done, or when your anxiety level is so high that you can't settle down to study for that exam. You will also need to know how to nurture the people you care about. Those who embark with you on your journey toward that diploma or certificate need to know that you understand how difficult it can get for them too. Rather than limit your expectations to what they can do for you, expect to continuously ask yourself what you can do to help them. If you support them, they will support you, and thus you'll establish a circular ongoing pattern of nurturing one another through school and other experiences. The ability to integrate new aspects of living with your old way of doing things includes being comforting, supportive, and deeply understanding of others.

Don't overdo the nurturing; too much concern for others may come across as the kind of overbearing and overprotective care that will cause them to wonder whether you trust them to take care of themselves. Being too good to yourself may result in excusing yourself too frequently from reasonable student responsibilities. You can choose to help yourself and those who are helping you and even enjoy the school experience.

Exercises

 Individual Activity

1. Make a list of all of the not-OK Critical Parent messages that are causing you to be unreasonably demanding and hard on yourself. Now determine where they came from in the first place and why you've been hanging on to them.
2. Make a list of your OK Critical Parent messages that you feel will help you through school. Where did these come from?
3. Make a list of what you have done to nurture yourself and others through new experiences. What can you do to help yourself and others through the school experience?

Class Discussion

Discuss the not-OK Critical Parent messages that students typically impose on themselves. You may want to share how you are being unreasonable with yourself. What are the OK Critical Parent messages that students know they should listen to? You may want to share what you are doing that is helping you and your family adjust to integrating your new student status with habitual patterns of daily living.

Small-Group Discussion

Help one another think of things you can do to nurture those who are going through this experience with you. Remember that what you do for them will undoubtedly enrich what they in turn do for you.

Class Discussion

Discuss what students typically expect of their spouses, children, relatives, friends, and lovers. Think of your own expectations of the people who are an important part of your life. What do you feel they should be doing for you? How much of this have you discussed with your family? How much has simply been an assumption either on your part or on their part?

Now discuss what you feel they can reasonably expect from you. Do they have a right to ask you to do things like cook, pick up groceries, take care of the kids, clean up the house, mow the lawn, go away for the weekend, and go out to dinner and a movie?

Also discuss what you feel are the needs of the important people in your life. How much should they modify their needs while you're a student?

Small-Group Activity

As a student you may or may not be holding down a job. Get together with people who are holding down jobs. Those who are not working should get together with others who are not working. Discuss how school may be interfering with your personal or work life. Share what you have done to solve the problems. Let the group help you analyze alternative approaches to the same problems.

You may find it helpful to form a group of three or four members as a support system to help you cope with on-the-job, off-the-job, and school- and home-related concerns.

Letting your *CHILD* educate you

Your Parent may set your goals for you, but, if your Natural Child isn't motivated by them, then your goals will very likely not materialize. You may force yourself to believe that you are excited about where you're going and make yourself go through all of the motions of getting there—such as spending long hours studying, attending all of the required courses, and doing all of the required assignments—but somehow fall short of receiving that diploma or certificate. You may even go ahead and graduate but find yourself looking for jobs outside your field. Or you may actually find yourself in the middle of a career you never wanted, doing work that reflects your half-hearted attitude.

Students often neglect to pay attention to their gut-level feelings, in the belief that, as long as their Parent tells them what to do and the Adult handles the details, they're going to make it through school. They may either go out of their way to suppress their Natural Child just to ensure that their feelings don't interfere with their schooling and stick with Parent-imposed goals that don't really interest them or allow their Natural Child to play all the time and eventually flunk out. What good is it to "make it through school" or to "work at flunking out" when at the end of all that time there is nothing that you really want to do? Perhaps you should ask yourself:

"Am I choosing to ignore my gut-level feelings?"
"Why am I doing this?"
"Am I afraid that if I listen to my Natural Child I may end up setting different goals for myself than those I *should* want?"
"What would happen if I do change my goals?"

In addition to being afraid to find out what they really want to specialize in, students ignore their Natural Child for still another reason. This Child is often equated with "being irresponsible," and, since the last thing students need is to feel irresponsible, they often go out of their way to eliminate or suppress deep feelings and emotions. Such self-control may create an illusion of accomplishment and responsibility, but it is only an illusion. If the Natural Child does not come out to play, relax, and express deep emotions once in a while, tension and stress build up and often result in loss of health, irritability, and an inability to cope.

You don't have to let your Natural Child run your student life; some students do just that and suddenly find themselves flunking out of school. Instead you can choose when to let yourself play and when to buckle down to study. Just as you must learn self-control, so you must learn how to give yourself room for fun. Whenever you give your Natural Child time out to express and play, you are communicating something very important to the significant people in your life. You are actually showing them with your behavior that it's also OK for them to have fun and to release frustration. Helping yourself and others free up the Natural Child in order to relieve the pressures of striving toward goals will help make those goals achievable.

Since your Natural Child needs the opportunity to express your unique individuality, you can also allow it to participate in school projects and papers. You can learn how to assert your own point of view during class discussions and to contribute your honest opinions in committee work. Paying attention to your gut-level feelings can also help you recognize your own unique learning style. By looking at the courses you enjoy, you can figure out what it is about them that you like.

Do you prefer courses that require term papers and no exams, those that require essay exams, or those that stress objective tests and no papers? Are experimental courses that place little emphasis on exams or written work your favorite? In other words, how do you like to learn? If you can figure this out, then you can pick and choose to take courses designed in a way that complements your learning style. You can also pay attention to what time of the day you learn best and whenever possible select to take courses offered during those hours.

Unfortunately you won't be able to get into the courses you want all of the time. Your program may require that you take some courses that you don't want to take, some that seem irrelevant to your major, and some that don't complement your style of learning. More often than not, however, if you pay attention to yourself, the courses offered, and those who teach them, you will be able to enroll in classes that your Natural Child enjoys.

Although you do want to give yourself plenty of room for open and genuine self-expression, your Adaptive Child's need for acceptance will temper that. Your Adaptive Child generally wants to obey such orders as:

> "Don't make a fool of yourself in class."
> "Don't take a course that may upset your grade-point average."
> "Make sure that you please your teachers."
> "Make sure that you get good grades."

This Child may, then, keep you from enrolling in a course that you want to take but have not taken due to fear of exploring new territories. If you have always enjoyed music and would really like to take music lessons or a course in music theory, your Adaptive Child may talk you out of doing it because:

> "It's been so long since I've tried something new."
> "I'm afraid that I won't be any good at it."
> "I'm afraid to start from scratch."
> "All the students in my classes will already know how to read music, and they will be way ahead of me."
> "I may get a low grade."

Perhaps you can convince yourself to be adventurous with at least one course; even if you don't perform well, it won't affect your overall grade point average greatly, nor will it keep you from fulfilling your desired goals. You will, however, have made a difference in your life: you will have faced a challenge you had never tried before, without having any idea of the outcome.

Your eager-to-please nature can stifle you, but, if you choose to, you can instead use your adaptive qualities to help you listen more attentively in class, take a little extra time to go over your assignments, work harder toward earning better grades, and meet deadlines. Since your degree of adaptiveness is equal to how much respect you're willing to give others and how much you're willing to compromise yourself, it's important that you not allow your Adaptive Child to overpower your need to be natural. Those students who continually try to be perfect are allowing their Adaptive Child to work overtime and most likely won't use the school experience to explore and to challenge themselves. Instead they will stay on familiar ground, in courses and extracurricular activities that are safe.

As a student you can also benefit from your creative Little Professor, for it is this Child that comes up with exceptional ideas, discovers how to add that unusual point of view, and knows how to get things done quickly and efficiently. This Child is alert to how to achieve the recognition you want, how to please teachers and others who are helping you with your education, and finally how to make the seemingly impossible become reality.

Being a student is not easy, and it can be unbearable if the Adaptive Child suppresses natural needs or is afraid to allow the Little Professor to be fully creative. Knowing how to use the Child ego state constructively has helped many students have an exciting and enjoyable learning experience. Are you willing to give yourself that kind of an education?

Exercises

Class Discussion

It may be helpful for class members to talk about what students often find stressful and how they cope with high-anxiety situations. Sometimes finding out what makes others feel uncomfortable and pressured and discovering that you have those pressures in common helps to relieve stress. Discuss the following:

1. What is typically stressful to students?
2. How can a person use his or her Natural Child to relieve stress?
3. What can people do to help others who are struggling through the student experience with them to bring out their Natural Child?

Small-Group Activity

Discuss what you consider to be acceptable and helpful natural behavior in committee work and during class discussion.

Now discuss what you consider to be obnoxious behavior, and without using names describe students and teachers who you feel have come across as *too* Natural. You may find that what you consider to be an extreme is really acceptable behavior to others.

Individual Activity

How do you like to learn—that is, what is your unique learning style? Find out whose teaching style matches your learning style. What are some courses that your Natural Child would like to try out but your Adaptive Child is shying away from? What is motivating your Adaptive Child to avoid trying out something new?

"How do I reason through getting there?" 23

Letting your ADULT

educate you

"Getting there" is one thing, but being well prepared to handle your career and goals once you finish school is quite another. Students have been know to "ace" exams and courses to graduate with honors but retain little practical knowledge for future use. The learning process need not be one of rote memorization. Memorizing facts and retaining them long enough to pass exams is not how one goes about turning facts into a practical, useful data base. Students need to constantly think through what they learn to discover how they can apply their learning to real-life situations. They may start by asking themselves, their teachers, and fellow students such questions as:

> "How can I apply this knowledge today, tomorrow, and in the future?"
> "What are the specific real-life situations for which I lack sufficient data?"
> "What is it that I need to know that I don't even know to ask about?"
> "Can I apply this information in such-and-such a situation, and what will happen if I do?"

Your Adult is only as responsible as you allow yourself to be. A well-functioning Adult doesn't simply obtain the kind of information that will get you through school, although it is important, but rather adopts a broader frame of mind. Broader vision includes gaining a good understanding of what exactly you plan to do once you graduate and what you will need as a data base in order to feel prepared to handle those responsibilities.

A good data base consists not only of the kind of information that will help you function well in your career but also of the kind that will help you function well interpersonally on and off the job. Interpersonal skills are not limited to problem-solving and communication strategies but also include being able to converse about a variety of subjects. No matter where you are, there are always people who are seeking others with whom they can discuss such topics as literature, the arts, politics, history, and philosophy. Your Adult knows that, in addition to selecting elective courses that complement your career, it's wise to round out your education with interesting electives in other areas. An education can be used to prepare you for a job. It can also be used to prepare you for people and pleasure.

The future is an important consideration for students and should influence what they do in school. But, while in school, students can rely on their Adult to help them meet day-to-day student responsibilities. More and more students find themselves ill prepared for the courses they're attempting to cope with. Their data base may be deficient either because they've been out of school for a long time and have forgotten much of what they had learned or because they're coming straight from high school with reading, writing, or math deficiencies. Since most schools offer refresher courses not only in the basics but also in speed-reading, study skills, typing, and shorthand, it seems logical to find out what exactly your deficiencies are and to fill in those gaps. This is not to say that every student should know how to type or speed-read, but failure to resolve basic reading, writing, and math deficiencies will make it difficult to keep up with course work, which in turn will make it almost impossible to cope with off-campus commitments. The faster you read and comprehend what you've read, the quicker you'll finish assignments and the more time you'll have for other things you have or want to do.

A contaminated Adult, however, can set you back every time you're trying to get ahead. Conflicting and confusing Parent contamination may cause you to think "I don't have to study; I never even opened a book in high school." Child contamination is equally risky: "All I have to do is use my charm on my teachers and show up in class and they'll pass me." You should know better, but, if you don't, then experience may have to be your teacher.

The combination of your uncontaminated Adult and Little Professor working together can result in outstanding achievement. Putting creativity together with good data will more than likely result in self-expression that is unique and relevant. Another good combination is your Adaptive Child and your uncontaminated Adult. Adapting yourself in order to pay close attention to classroom instructions is great, but it is not as useful as being able to pick out the important points. You can't possibly absorb all of the information you're exposed to in one sitting, but you can use your Adult to distinguish between what are and what are not important data.

Your Natural Child may want to express your ideas in class, but combining that Child with your uncontaminated Adult will help you to say what's relevant and to the point.

Also, there is something to be gained from combining your OK Parent with your Adult. Your OK Critical Parent may be giving you good advice, but your Adult can help you use that advice in an appropriate manner. It's good to know that you have to study, but knowing when and how to study efficiently and effectively will increase your productivity. Your uncontaminated Adult can help regulate the amount of nurturing you derive from that OK Parent, when you need it, and when you need to be giving it to others. The idea is to use your uncontaminated Adult as your balance point or referee between the other ego states in order to bring out the best of each. Your Adult may be rusty, but it knows that the more you practice, the better you will be able to reason. School is an ideal situation that, if well used, will enable you to oil, polish, and test-run your uncontaminated Adult until you feel that it's in good enough shape and has the power to tackle different environments and situations.

Exercise

Check out what your deficiencies are. Do you need refresher courses in math, reading, or English? Could you use a speed-reading course? What about a course in shorthand or typing? Study skills?

Find out whether or not your school offers tutorial services. Most schools make these available at no cost to the student.

Does your school offer study-skills workshops?

Find out how to use the library. Either an English teacher or librarian or an experienced fellow student or tutor may be able to help you.

Letting your EGO-STATE PORTRAIT

educate you

Getting there requires that your Parent establish reasonable demands, that your Adult keep tabs on what needs to be done, and that your Child remain enthusiastic about your goals. In order to maintain such a balance among your ego states, you'll have to learn how to meet daily challenges with a balanced ego-state portrait. In the introduction to this section of the book we looked at situations that often plague students. Let's look at these typical concerns one by one and become acquainted with "balanced" versus the Parent-, Child-, or Adult-dominant approach to problem solving.

1. *How do I cope with the grievances of my neglected spouse?* Your spouse confronts you with: "All you ever do is study. We never have fun anymore." "If I'm going to support you through school, you'd better not take me for granted." You can choose to respond as follows:

Parent-dominant:	"All you ever do is complain. Can't you understand that what I'm doing is important and that I'm doing this for us?"
Child-dominant:	This student has obviously neglected the Child in his or her spouse. This doesn't mean, however, that the student isn't partying and letting his or her Child out with fellow students.
Adult-dominant:	"Before this quarter ends, I have to finish two papers and study for three finals. This doesn't leave any time to play."

Balanced portrait:	"I got so caught up with what I have to do for school that I forgot about us. Studying as hard as I've been studying for so long is bound to have negative effects. I need to remember that we both need time to 'refuel.' So let's go out tonight and take a break. We both deserve it."

2. *How do I cope with family demands,* such as: "Thanksgiving is a family tradition, and, exams or not, we expect you to be here." You can choose to respond as follows:

Parent-dominant:	"Don't boss me around. You always do that."
Child-dominant:	"I don't want to come home for Thanksgiving, and you can't make me. If you want to cut off my allowance, just go ahead and see if I care."
Adult-dominant:	"There is no time for a Thanksgiving break until I graduate, because finals are always right after Thanksgiving and I can't allow time for pleasure."
Balanced portrait:	"Yes, I'll be home for Thanksgiving dinner, but, since I have finals immediately after the break, I will be bringing my books home with me and studying most of the time while I'm at home." Or "No, I won't be coming home for Thanksgiving because I'll be too worried about my finals, and you know that I can't study at home. I have, however, already made plans to come home for Christmas, and I'm looking forward to seeing you."

3. *How do I cope with "Odd Couple" roommate problems,* such as: "What do you mean, you're 'having a few friends drop in tonight'? I've got an exam in the morning!" If you're the one who has invited the friends over, you can choose to respond as follows:

Parent-dominant:	"You should know better than to keep secrets. Why didn't you tell me that you had an exam coming up? If I had known, I wouldn't have invited company for tonight."
Child-dominant:	"Oh, come on, don't worry about that exam tonight. You can worry about it in the morning. So c'mon and party with us."
Adult-dominant:	"We will be in the living room, and you will be in the bedroom. We do not plan to be noisy. You will therefore not be bothered by us."
Balanced portrait:	"I am sorry about the fact that you didn't warn me about your exam and that I didn't warn you about the fact that I wanted to have a few people over tonight. Let's make sure that we keep each other better informed in the future. Now, let's decide what we can do to resolve the problem. I could take my party to the pub, or you could go to the library for the evening."

4. *How do I learn to discipline myself so that I can behave differently than:* "Oh well, so I flunk another exam. Let's start the party!"

Parent-dominant:	This individual needs to develop his or her OK Critical Parent. The Parent ego state is obviously underdeveloped.
Child-dominant:	That's the problem. This individual is allowing his or her Natural Child to dominate his or her coping strategies.
Adult-dominant:	This individual has chosen to ignore his or her Adult data.
Balanced portrait:	This individual needs to develop OK Critical Parent messages in order to make the Natural Child adopt some Adaptive qualities and conform to strategies that will enable him or her to realize designated goals. If the goals

that have been set are not something
that the student is looking forward to,
then this person's Natural Child will not
listen to any Parent messages.

As you can see, different portraits result in different problem-
solving strategies and consequently also in different life-styles. The
life-style of a Parent-dominant individual is going to be quite different
from that of a Child-dominant or Adult-dominant person. An individual
with a balanced ego-state portrait can learn how to reap the benefits
from all three ego states and combine them to lead a life that is balanced
among the Parent, Adult, and Child.

Exercise

The following class activity will help you learn to distinguish
between how the different portraits cope with everyday student
problems.

As a class, give examples of how a balanced portrait versus
a Parent-, Child-, or Adult-dominant portrait would cope with
the following situations. Follow the format used throughout
this chapter.

1. How do I help my children understand that spending less
   time with them doesn't mean that I love them less?
2. How do I cope with professors who intimidate me?
3. How do I cope with employers who are not as understanding as I hoped they would be?
4. How do I cope with my friends who insist on calling me
   during my study hours even though I've asked them not to?
5. Suggest your own problem situation.

"How can my attitude help me get there?" **25**

Letting your POSITION educate you

Identifying your goal and understanding what you'll have to do to reach it isn't enough to get yourself started or to finish what you've started. Your Parent may tell you what you should do and your Adult may know how to do it, but, unless you feel that you *can* accomplish what you set out to do, then you probably will find a way to excuse yourself from making a commitment to a goal. It's important, therefore, that, before you approach anything, you're able to say "Not only do I want to do it, but also I feel that I can do it." This is the same as adopting the I'm OK, You're (my goal) is OK position, or "I can do it, and I want to do it." The self-defeating alternatives are:

"I can't do it even though I want to do it." (I'm not-OK, my goal is OK)

"I can't do it, and I also don't want to do it." (I'm not-OK, my goal is not-OK)

"I can do it, but I don't want to do it." (I'm OK, my goal is not-OK)

Let's look at these positions more closely.

"I Can Do It, and I Want to Do It."

If you have adopted this position, you are fortunate indeed. For not only have you identified what your Parent has approved, your Adult has researched, and your Child is excited about, but you also see yourself as qualified to achieve your undertaking. This means that your goal is neither over your head nor something that you really aren't very

172

excited about doing. You're not fighting against yourself, and you're not fighting against your goal. You are, therefore, in a position to get there. Getting there is important to you, and you know that you will reach your goal, but you're also flexible enough to say:

> "I wanted that A, but I learned a lot even though I got a B."
> "I wanted my starting salary to be higher, but since this is the job I really want, I am willing to settle for a lesser salary."
> "I know that I have many things to do, but I will take one thing at a time."
> "I know what it takes to get there, but I won't ignore my Child or anyone else's Child in the process."

"I Can't Do It Even Though I Want to Do It."

If you have adopted this position, either you are competent but lacking in self-confidence to get you going or you may be the kind who typically selects goals that are over your head. You therefore set yourself up not to accomplish what you set out to do. In either case you shortchange yourself. In checking out your ego-state portrait you may find that your Child is dominating you with fear of failure or fear of success, that your Adult hasn't taken the steps to select goals you can handle, and that your Parent has you believing that you can't finish what you start. You may find yourself lamenting:

> "Poor me, I wish that I could be _____, but I just know that I won't make it."
> "I wish that I could have _____, but I don't have what it takes to get it. I want to do well in _____, but I always fall short of my goal."
> "Others told me that I should pursue this goal. This goal is worthwhile, so why am I so unhappy."

"I Can't Do It, and I Also Don't Want to Do It."

You not only see yourself as unable or unmotivated to achieve anything, but also you may believe that there isn't a goal out there that's worth caring about. If you do set a goal, it's probably only because someone has forced you or is prodding you to do so. The position that "I can't do it, and I don't want to do it" puts you in double jeopardy; in this position you have removed all possibility for being internally or externally motivated. You have resigned yourself to the fact that you don't have what it takes and, even if you did, there's nothing out there you want very much anyway. Thus you totally immobilize yourself.

Your ego-state portrait is probably dominated by the not-OK Critical Parent, your Adult is more than likely either decommissioned or contaminated, and your Child has very likely adopted an "I don't care" attitude.

"I Can Do It, but I Don't Want to Do It."

You may feel that you can do anything you put your mind to but that there isn't a goal that's worthy of your time and energy. Or you may feel qualified to reach the goal you have undertaken but resentful because that goal was forced on you. In either case, there isn't enough drive in you to get you going, let alone get you there. If you're the first type, you may find that you start many things but never finish them. Whenever you're strongly attracted to something, you may jump into it with high energy but very quickly become disillusioned. It's as if your life consists of jumping from one thing to another without quite knowing what's really happening to you. You may, in fact, be camouflaging fear of failure with the attitude "Nothing is good enough for me."

If you're the second type, you're allowing yourself to be manipulated into doing what you "should" be doing rather than what you want to be doing. Since you know better, then you need to ask yourself:

> "Why am I doing this to myself?"
> "Who am I doing this for?"
> "What's it going to do to me if I continue to do this to myself?"

Some individuals adopt this position because they feel they have been shortchanged in life and that someone out there owes them something. This person may see the self as OK, but his or her resentment puts a barrier between the self and anyone or anything else. This type may sound like this:

> "I show up for your classes and hand in assignments. What else do you want from me?"
> "I bring home a pay check. What else do you want?"

"I'm majoring in what you wanted me to major in. What else do you want?"
"You have the pleasure of my company. Why aren't you grateful?"

Your attitude or position will make a difference in school or any time you're trying to achieve a goal. It will affect whether or not you graduate and whether or not you'll succeed in your career. Future goals are achieved not by wishing for them but by actively taking yourself and your responsibilities into your own two hands, gaining a clear understanding of the steps you need to go through to get there, and taking on the plan with a positive attitude about yourself and your goal.

In Chapter 10, the seven-step action plan was used to demonstrate an attitude change. If you're dissatisfied with your position toward school or your personal or work-related responsibilities, you can use that plan to actively change your position.

Exercise

Identify your current position and write it down.

How do you know that this is your position? Write down your behaviors and feelings that are indicative of the position you're currently supporting.

If you haven't already done so, would you like to adopt the "I can make it, and I want to make it" position? Now state how you think that position would change your life.

You may already be operating from the I'm OK, and my goal is OK position. Write down why you like it. Now state how you can polish that position so that it can work even better for you.

Letting your SCRIPT educate you

When we talk about coping with the personal, school, and work-related worlds, we can distinguish between informal or personal time and institutionalized or organized time. You basically set your own rules in your personal world and follow rules in the other two. Thus, coping strategies reflect the degree of your control and power over your environments. For most people, the first exposure to an institutionalized setting is school. When we start school, we learn about what it means to cooperate with total strangers and what it takes to befriend them and fit them into our lives. The coping strategies you learned in the first few years of school can probably be referred to as your organization script, or how you feel you should behave in order to fit into institutions. Let's take a look at how you may have developed interpersonal behavior patterns in school that you later ended up taking to work and to other organized settings with you.

You probably started attending some type of school between age 4 and age 6, and, in becoming a little student, you stepped into a brand new life experience. Your world suddenly included many more people and a completely new environment. The concepts of teacher, student, and classroom slowly took shape, and, as you started interacting with and coping with this new world, you developed feelings and attitudes toward it and more importantly toward yourself. At some point you decided that school was an "OK" place to be and that teachers and students were "OK" people. Or you decided the opposite. This decision evolved out of school-related experiences that culminated in OK or not-OK feelings. And, as these experiences multiplied, you started feeling OK or not-OK about yourself. You brought a personal life script to school with you and reinforced or reworked it to reflect your new environment. You may even have developed two separate scripts—one for home and one for school. In any case, you adopted and started to follow your script or scripts, with the firm conviction that that's just the way things are.

As you became aware of the meaning of competing for attention in school, your ability to compete with fellow students helped you decide to seek recognition, either constructively or destructively. The in-between world seemed least desirable because that's where no one noticed you. Since positive recognition is more desirable, you worked hard for it. When you got it, you felt really OK about yourself and school. As a result you confirmed that you fit into the school setting, that you felt competent, and that you enjoyed working cooperatively. Today, you may still be thriving on group involvement.

On the other hand, you may have discovered that your behavior in school didn't get your teacher's or even your fellow students' stamp of approval, so you backed off and became an observer rather than a participant. This self-exclusion reflected an embarrassing moment, a first-time experience you dealt with inappropriately, or something very positive that you didn't know how to accept. You lacked adaptive skills and therefore may have seen yourself as not-OK in an environment that others seemed to be enjoying. You may have adopted that self-image during your early school experiences and still have it today.

That in-between world where you went unnoticed may not have suited you. The payoffs weren't gratifying. Your developing Adult was aware of what it took to "fit in," and your Little Professor began to find shortcuts to positive recognition. This is when you may have discovered how to cheat or copy from successful students' papers or how to imitate interpersonal coping strategies that seemed to work for other students.

Your new behavior may have been "fake"; that is, you may have forced yourself to adopt the behavior patterns you thought you should follow. Was it your teacher's pleasant surprise at your improved performance or the general acceptance of your behavior that confirmed that that's how you play the organizational game? If it worked for you then, you may still be playing that kind of "fitting" game today.

You may have been unlucky with that self-compromising strategy, and others may have rebuffed you with "Stop acting stupid." "Can't you be yourself?" At this point you may have become confused and, not knowing how to behave, again retreated into that in-between world and remained there to this day.

That lack of attention, however, may not have been any better than the first time, and it probably wasn't long before you discovered that destructive and annoying behavior also got you attention. It was negative attention, but it felt better than being ignored. Having successfully manipulated your environment to get the attention you wanted may have resulted in feelings of "I'm OK after all, but those administrators, teachers and students, and even my parents who keep pushing me are not-OK." At this point you may have confirmed that the only way to matter was to rebel against authority figures. So you put your Little Professor in charge. Your "acting out" coping strategy may still be with you today.

If, however, you came face-to-face with authority figures who did not tolerate this acting out and who openly singled you out for punishment and rejection, you felt that life was pretty miserable at school and you never wanted to go back again. But you lost that battle and had to go back. Your decision this time to retreat probably emerged with rage as you lost the battle and therefore felt that you were OK but were stuck in a not-OK environment. If you couldn't get attention for trying to fit in or for acting out, you may have decided to rebel by not learning at all. But, to your surprise, that behavior got you all kinds of special attention. The entire adult population was suddenly trying to motivate you to learn again, and the harder they tried, the less you learned. But at last you felt OK about yourself and even OK about them, because all that attention was forthcoming. If that worked for you then, it may still be working for you today.

Children who are learning to cope in the school environment are motivated to adopt and maintain coping strategies that get them the attention they want. Their ego-state portrait and position will reflect that "organization" script. What works for them initially is usually maintained throughout life. Most people feel too vulnerable to put themselves in a position to try out new behavior. They won't do so unless what has previously worked isn't working anymore.

Exercises

 Are you aware of your organization script? The following exercises will help you clarify how you're currently coping in organized settings and how you will probably continue to work with others unless you decide to change or alter your script.

Individual Activity

Whenever people adopt an organization script, they also

adopt a set of behaviors to support that script. Think about when you first decided:

1. to like school/not to like school;
2. to speak in front of a group/never again to speak in front of a group;
3. to create pretty pictures/never to draw again;
4. to come up with original ideas/not to think for yourself;
5. to trust fellow students/not to trust anyone;
6. to like teachers/to dislike teachers or authority figures;
7. to trust yourself/not to trust yourself;
8. to get good grades/never again to try for good grades;
9. to eat lunch with the group/to eat lunch alone;
10. to excel in physical education/to avoid physical activity;
11. to please others/to annoy others;
12. to work cooperatively/to be a rebel.

Now go back to each item and see whether you can remember why you made that decision in the first place. Would you like to re-decide and take a chance on a "new you," a new organization script? What would living that new script be like?

Class Activity

Discuss what you feel to be good organization behavior, and support your point of view. If you could write the "ideal" organization script, what would it be?

Letting your STROKES
educate you

Somewhere in your past—perhaps the recent past—you have probably heard yourself saying "Why does everyone tell me what to do? I can't even turn around without having someone at my heels or leading me by the hand telling me how, when, and what to do. I can't stand it! Why can't they just leave me alone! If they would only quit bugging me, I could prove that I can think on my own and be responsible for myself." These are often complaints of the teenager who is still being protected by others and wants very much to be self-controlling. Do you remember when you last felt overprotected to the point where you thought "It's not that they want to take care of me—it's that they don't trust me."

You either already have found or will soon find yourself in an environment where such nudging and urging is hard to come by. Typically, such attention doesn't exist in post-high school education or in most work environments. This is not to say that, when you go to college, to vocational training institutions, or to work, you won't be inundated with rules, regulations, and responsibilities. What it does mean is that very rarely will someone be standing over you to make sure that you get things done or take extra time with you to show you how to do them.

Once you graduate from high school you're going to find that you're basically on your own, and you therefore need to know how to be self-motivated and how to ask for help. Otherwise, you may not accomplish what you set out to do. Those in your past who pushed you along more than likely believed that they were supporting you with positive stroking. If you don't recall such stroking, it's probably because

you saw it as negative stroking, preceded or followed by a statement
such as:

> "You don't appreciate what I'm trying to do for you."
> "You don't know what's good for you."
> "Some day you'll be glad that I made you do that."
> "Don't ask any questions—just do what I tell you to do!"

College is an environment where rules, regulations, and responsibilities exist in abundance but where you're on your own when it comes
to finding out how to do things. Unless you take the initiative and ask for
assistance, teachers, administrators, and other students won't be there
for you. College professors tend to operate on the assumption that you
are responsible for when, how, and what you do; if you can't help
yourself or ask for help, then that's your problem.

Once a professor hands you a course outline, you may be
completely on your own. It's up to you to decide what you are going to
put into the courses, how you're going to meet the course requirements,
and when you're going to devote time to that class. Often it's up to you
even to decide whether you're going to show up for class, take notes,
study for exams, and write required papers.

When you're stuck, you may find one of your fellow students to
help you out, provided it's not going to take too much time. They're
quite busy, too, trying to get things done. For the first time you may
actually miss those people who watched over every step you took. Your
parents may not even want to help you; if they went to college, they
may feel that that's where they were exposed to the "sink or swim" men-
tality. Since they had to make it on their own, they may now expect you
to do so.

But what if you don't know how to ask for help, how to study,
how to manage your time, how to write term papers, how to use the
library—in short, how to be a responsible student? What then?

Don't Panic! In most colleges there is a way to get the kind of
assistance you need. Not only are there trained counselors available to
help you with your personal and career-search concerns, but also there
are free peer-tutorial services available. Peer tutors are students who
help other students on a one-to-one or group basis with their academic
and adjustment problems. Most colleges even offer full-credit courses
designed to help you identify your personal, vocational, and educational
goals and ways of reaching them. And don't forget that refresher course
in math, reading, or English, not to mention speed-reading, typing, and

shorthand that are yours for the taking. One way to give yourself positive strokes is to make use of such facilities.

College may be a "sink or swim" kind of place, but obviously there are all kinds of help available if you take the time to look for it. This is true in practically all situations where groups of people congregate to work, learn, or play together. Just ask around or look for printed information on the kinds of facilities available to you, and then make use of them.

So there is help available to you. As a matter of fact, this help is unconditional—yours for the asking. You may have to fill out forms and, if the facility services many people, put your name on a waiting list. But don't let that stop you from getting the help you want. The mistake most people make is that they don't even think about making use of the facilities that are available to them until a crisis situation panics them. They may seek out a peer tutor when it's too late (a week before the exam); they may seek marital counseling after they've decided to get a divorce; or they may go to a hospital after their nose has healed crookedly so that it has to be rebroken.

It's important to keep in mind that a systematic check-and-balance system will help you take care of problems before they hit the panic point. Doctors and dentists urge systematic checkups, teachers urge systematic study patterns, employers look for systematic daily progress, and families look for ongoing affection. What do you look for in yourself? Keep in mind that by learning how to help yourself you also put yourself in a position to help out others. Perhaps you can lend a nurturing hand to those who are beginning to go through what you have already mastered.

Exercise

 Your assignment is to check out the facilities that are available to help you at school, at work, and in the community. Make a list of where you can get the kind of help you may need, and keep it handy.

Letting effective *TIME STRUCTURING* educate you

How to structure time is an important issue for students. Students often complain about not having enough hours in a day to do what needs to be done. It's overwhelming enough for them to properly manage all that they have to accomplish for school, let alone to fit in other commitments such as family and job-related responsibilities. Rather than structuring time haphazardly and thus taking the risk of neglecting one responsibility for another and feeling overwhelmed by it all, students can choose to control their time efficiently and effectively. Let's look at how they can use such strategies as withdrawals, rituals, pastimes, activities, and games to excuse themselves from commitments and how they can use them to structure time to ensure that they include all that needs doing.

Using Withdrawals

Student responsibilities don't vanish; they hang on, multiply, and insist on being there regardless of where the student is. Students typically love to procrastinate and thus waste many valuable hours trying to decide whether to study. When they withdraw into thinking about what they want to do, they're neither studying nor doing other things. When they finally decide, they may find that it's too late to get started doing anything. This is when they waste even more time feeling sorry about the time they've just wasted. As a result they often find themselves cornered with much unfinished business and consequently see themselves as not-OK, irresponsible, and unable to live up to their commitments.

Withdrawing is not necessarily a negative behavior that works against students. It is not only healthy but also necessary to withdraw from commitments once in a while. You need to learn to schedule yourself so that you're in control of when you withdraw from your studies and when you withdraw from people. A pleasant fantasy diversion can temporarily relieve your mind from your obligations. Controlling when you take a break to relieve tension or relax your mind also puts you in command of when you devote your full attention to your responsibilities. Neither withdrawal tactics nor responsibilities have to have a hold on you; rather, you can be in charge of when you withdraw and when you tackle your commitments.

If, however, you can't seem to control when you withdraw but, rather, find yourself unable to keep your mind on what needs doing, then you may be forcing yourself to be responsible for something you really don't want to have any part of. This may include a particular course you're taking, your major as a whole, or outside pressures related to your job or private life. Another reason for such withdrawal is to have a Child within who is starved for attention, and still another is getting yourself into something that's over your head. When students find they are ill equipped for the responsibilities they've undertaken, they may find that, rather than deal with their skill deficiencies, they withdraw.

Using Rituals

Schools are ritualized institutions. There are the quarter and semester systems, there are football and basketball seasons, there are graduation exercises and class reunions, and there are codes of conduct and academic standards. The list is endless, for tradition is what builds an institution's reputation, and that's what attracts its students.

On a day-by-day basis students are involved in rituals such as scheduled classes, meetings, carpools, and meal times. Sometimes school-related rituals interfere with job-related or family-related traditions. If mealtime at home has always been at 6 P.M. and the club you've just joined always meets on Mondays at 6 P.M., you may have a problem.

Although rituals are very much a part of school life, students typically don't think of ritualizing their study time. Perhaps one of the most helpful ways to get yourself through school is to set aside specific hours during each and every day for study purposes and to stick to that schedule as much as possible.

Using Activities

Some students believe that, in order to make it through school, they must study all the time and therefore take little time out for other activities. There are many constructive activities, however, that allow students not only to relieve tension and frustrations but also to enrich their learning experience and to enjoy themselves. Students have access to school-sponsored extracurricular activities, and schools promote them because they feel that learning should not be limited to the classroom. Learning can and often does take place whenever students gather together.

Most schools encourage students to join career-oriented clubs such as journalism, debate, drama, and nurses' or teachers' clubs. They also provide students with the opportunity to participate in organized activities that emphasize physical development and coordination, such as cheerleading, football, tennis, fencing, judo, and dance. In addition they encourage student-government organizations and social committees that stress school parties, picnics, and trips. These are not only great outlets for the Natural Child but also terrific ways to meet people and perhaps develop lifelong friendships.

Using Pastimes

Students have often said that some of their best learning experiences have occurred during rap sessions. Those who live in dormitories, frequent student lounges, join fraternities and sororities, or enjoy pubs and cafés where students hang out can benefit greatly from exchanging ideas, venting frustrations, and simply enjoying the camaraderie. These pastimes can be ritualized in that some students plan to work hard all week and give themselves Saturday nights off to go to the disco. Carefully planning when to seek out such companionship is important; too much socializing can flunk you out of school and too much time spent studying can flunk you out socially.

Such pastimes provide an excellent opportunity for the student to bring spouses, dates, and friends into the school-related social scene. It can also give them a chance to see for themselves what students are concerned with and what they're learning about in school and to meet other nonstudents who are experiencing the same kind of life-style.

Using Games

Instead of playing avoidance games ("Why Don't You . . . ? Yes, But"), blaming games ("If it weren't for you" or "See what you made me do"), failure games ("See how hard I've tried" or "Wooden leg"), or anger and rebellion games ("Make Me!" or "Uproar"), why not play constructive games such as:

"How much do you want to bet that I *can* make it?"
"Ain't it useful!"
"See what I *can* do!"
"Look how well I can balance my time!"
"Success!"
"Why don't I take a chance on a course or club."
"Gold star!"
"I can make it!"

You can play constructive rather than destructive games, success and not failure games, and winner instead of loser games.

You can choose to control and balance your time between work and play. There's a "right" time to take care of school and other business, and there is a "right" time to escape into withdrawals, rituals, activities, pastimes, and games. The goal is to establish realistic and workable time frames for yourself daily, weekly, monthly, quarterly, and annually. When you have a clear picture of *all* that needs doing, then you can plan a schedule that will help you organize yourself in order to get things done. Some things need immediate attention, and others can wait. For example, people you're close to or living with may need your attention daily, but others can be enjoyed every few weeks. A daily study schedule is necessary, but a paper that's due at the end of the quarter or semester could be started three weeks prior to the due date. Daily physical exercise may be wise to schedule, but leave time-consuming major events such as tournaments for low-pressure times.

Exercise

 Draw up a chart to help you structure your time (See Table 28-1). In Chapter 24 you looked at your ego-state portrait, and you made a list of school-related, work-related, and personal responsibilities you have made a commitment to. Use that list for your chart.

Table 28-1.

Things I Have to Do	Daily	Weekly	Semi-Monthly	Monthly	Each Semester or Quarter	Annually	When Appropriate
Study	7:30–9:30	Sunday 9–5	study group	reviews	review session, conference with profs	read college catalog	exams papers presentations
Pay bills		groceries gas		rent car utilities phone	tuition insurance		doctors dentists
Take care of my child	take to school 8 A.M. pick up 3 P.M. play together 3–4:30	piano lessons	visit grandparents Saturday afternoon	whole-day adventure	family weekend	buy clothes	

Table 28-1, continued.

Things I Need to Do But Don't Have Time to Do	Daily	Weekly	Semi-Monthly	Monthly	Each Semester or Quarter	Annually	When Appropriate
Take care of house plants		water Saturday morning	plant food			trim re-pot	
Interior decorate							frame pictures for my office new drapes for family room defrost refrigerator
Housework	dishes	laundry grocery shopping dust	wash floors	yard work	windows clean out refrigerator	shampoo rug clean drapes	

Things I Want to Do	Daily	Weekly	Semi-Monthly	Monthly	Each Semester or Quarter	Annually	When Appropriate
Exercise	Jog 6:30–7:15 A.M.	4 miles		jog with friends		road race	
Entertainment	T.V. news	TV–Sunday 60 min.	Night out for just the 2 of us	gathering with friends	really plan to reward myself for the quarter	a week at the beach	Thanksgiving with family plan a party

Letting your *TRANSACTIONS*
educate you

Adjustment to any new situation can be stressful. Although the degree of stress varies with each individual and with each situation, one thing is certain: anyone who is experiencing such discomfort will aim to rid himself or herself of it. Before this stress is alleviated, however, it is usually communicated through verbal and nonverbal transactions.

Pressure does different things to different people. Some react with anger and quick temper, and others respond with silence and withdrawal tactics. Some constantly talk about their dilemma; others pretend that nothing out of the ordinary is happening and suddenly explode when they least expect it or when the worst is over. What's usually lurking behind stress is the fear of failure—"Will I make it?" Consequently, transactions that may ordinarily be complementary become crossed and ulterior. Analyzing such unexpected transactions and working toward uncrossing them may help to alleviate the strain and strife that come with stress.

Let's take a look at what fear can do to cross transactions or to make them ulterior. Fear is often related to not knowing how things are going to turn out. This not knowing causes people to speculate about what might happen: "If so-and-so does or says such-and-such, and then if I respond with . . . , then he or she will probably . . . ." They tend to feel that such rehearsals will give them greater control of situations that come up. The greater the fear, the more time is spent worrying and planning for future happenings. Unfortunately, much energy is spent on setting the self up with expectations that may not be realizable. Even if they are possible, the fantasy that has already been played in the mind will detract from what's really happening.

People may spend hours rehearsing what they'll say if someone says "No" to them, only to be surprised with a "yes." And then they'll spend even more time worrying about what that "yes" really meant. They may work themselves into a rage over what they expect someone to say or do, and, if the worst actually happens, they're already so angry that they are more than likely not going to handle the situation very well. Trying to outguess and rehearse for the future may not help you cope with it any better, but it does distract you from living in the here and now. Living for what might be, therefore, may keep you from fully experiencing and fully living life.

This is not to say that you shouldn't plan for the future; resigning yourself fully to the here and now with an attitude that says "Why plan anything? Everything is so unpredictable anyway" can also set you up for much disappointment. It may be pointless to rehearse specific conversations that might come up or to dwell on what you will do in a given situation, but it may be a mistake to give up control over major issues such as career and life-style.

The kinds of unconstructive rehearsals students may find themselves in may include:

> "What if I don't finish my paper on time?"
> "What if she really didn't mean what she said?"
> "What if I flunk the exam?"
> "What if I ask him to go to the party and he turns me down?"
> "What if he says yes?"
> "What if my car breaks down?"
> "What if I get sick?"

All of these "What if's" can and do come up. As a matter of fact, you have probably already experienced such "if's" numerous times. It's therefore appropriate that you ask yourself:

> "Did all of my worrying make any difference in how things turned out?"
> "Are people so predictable that I can count on my fantasy about them to come true?"
> "Could I have handled the situation better without my prerehearsed expectations?"
> "Can I learn to trust myself to handle situations spontaneously?"
> "Can I rely on my ego-state portrait, life position, and life script to handle transactions constructively as they come up?"

If you respect your values, trust your gut-level feelings, and have confidence in your data base; if your attitude allows you to be relaxed and open with yourself and others; and if your behavior shows self-respect and respect for others, then you are well prepared to handle anything that comes your way. If this is true for you, then whenever you find yourself worrying about "if's," remind yourself that you're wasting time and energy.

Why worry about "What if I don't get my paper in on time?" when you have the power to schedule yourself so that you do get your paper in on time.

Why worry about "What if she really didn't mean what she said?" when you can, in fact, ask her if she meant what she said.

Why worry about "What if I flunk the exam?" when you know that it's your responsibility to acquire proper study skills and to schedule yourself to have sufficient study time so that you don't flunk the exam.

Why worry about "What if I ask him to go to the party and he turns me down?" when you can logically assume that he has that option and may choose it. And, if he says no, the only negative consequence is your own self-persecution, which you can select not to engage in.

Why worry about "What if he says yes?" when you can choose to know yourself well enough to trust your behavior.

Why worry about "What if my car breaks down?" when you know that you can manage if it does break down.

Why worry about "What if I get sick?" when you know that sooner or later you probably will and that you can handle the situation when it comes up.

Exercise

 Take the time to talk about the "if's" that have been troubling you lately. As a group, help one another identify whether worrying about these "if's" will make any difference. Also discuss what that worrying may be doing to the worrier on a daily basis. Allow the worrier to decide whether he or she would like to continue worrying about that "if," and have him or her explain what it is about that "if" that requires that he or she continue to hang on to it.

Letting the SEVEN-STEP ACTION PLAN educate you

You have already applied the seven-step action plan to an interpersonal concern and to an interpersonal/vocational concern. You have seen how specifying an attitude change also requires that you work on your behavior and how changing your behavior also instigates an attitude change. In this final chapter, let's look at how you can go about changing an *intrapersonal* concern or one that involves your own behavior or attitude rather than what's going on between you and someone else.

As you look at your behavior, you may find that you would like to improve your reading skills, that you want to quit that cigarette habit, or that you want to learn how to study for longer periods of time. As you look at your attitudes, you may find that you want to change how you feel about spending more time by yourself, that you would like to work on procrastination, or that you would like to acquire a different attitude about health foods and exercise. Regardless of how many behaviors or attitudes you would like to change, select only one at a time to work on.

You may find it helpful to follow the action plan as we attempt to solve the following problem: "How can I learn how to study for longer periods of time?"

1. Identify Your Goal

If you want to increase the amount of time you spend studying, you will first have to clearly establish how much time you are currently devoting to studies. Once you identify where you are, you can clearly state where you would like to be. If you find that you are devoting an hour a day to your studies, then you can look at all of your other responsibilities and logically establish how much you can increase that time. Once you have established how much time you can devote to school work, you can state that as your goal: "I want to be able to study for two hours at a time every day during the week and two hours in the mornings and two hours in the afternoons on the weekends."

Now state your goal. First, state how long, how much, how many, or how frequently you're currently doing the behavior you would like to change. Second, state how long, how much, how many, or how frequently you would like to be doing this behavior in the future. For example, in the case of quitting smoking you may state that you're currently smoking 25 cigarettes a day and would like to cut that down to no cigarettes a day.

2. Understand Your Goal

What is the current undesirable situation that is making me want to increase how long I study?
   1. I have enough time to read my assignments but not enough to go back and study what I have read.
   2. I realize that I need to learn how to study for at least two hours with perhaps a five-minute break in between, because I'm not able to get my work done with my current study habits.
   3. I'm not doing as well as I'd like in my classes, and I know that I can improve that.
   4. I know that I'm in the habit of sitting still for an hour, but I can increase that to two hours.
   5. The papers I hand in show little thought and practically no creativity.
   6. I'm wasting a lot of time watching television when I could be studying instead.

What's motivating me to deal with this problem now?
   1. I'm starting a new quarter, and I want better grades than I got last quarter.
   2. I want to get more out of my education than simply passing courses. I want a data base I can use in the future.
   3. My self-image is suffering because of my poor grades.
   4. I want to have greater control over how I schedule my time.
   5. I don't want to disappoint my parents again.

What am I going to gain by reaching this goal?
   1. Better grades.

2. Greater self-esteem.
3. Proud parents.
4. A sense of accomplishment.
5. The knowledge that I can, in fact, alter my habits.
6. An education I can use in the future.

Now it's your turn to ask yourself these questions about your goal.

3. Take Full Responsibility for Reaching Your Goal

Now that you understand what you have been doing and what you would like to be doing instead, are you prepared to set out to reach your goal with an "I can do it" attitude? Can you think of anything that might keep you from achieving your goal? Would it be helpful to you to form a support group?

4. Describe Your Action Plan and Set Time Limits

What am I going to do to start working on my goal?
1. I am going to locate a quiet place that will become my study nook. I will always study in the same place. I will not do anything but study in my study nook.
2. Whenever I'm through studying, I will clean up and organize my materials so that I don't have to face a messy desk the next day.
3. I will have all of the necessary study equipment handy, including pencils, pens, paper, stapler, typewriter, and the like.
4. I will make sure that my desk is not facing a window. In other words, I will not allow myself to be distracted in any way.
5. I will not watch TV or listen to music while I study.
6. I will post a calendar in my study nook on which I will record all of my due dates and scheduled exams. This calendar will also include other plans.
7. I will set aside two-hour blocks for study purposes every

day, and I will pencil them in on my calendar. I may have to reschedule some of my other plans, but if I can't then I'll schedule my two-hour study block around them. One thing is certain, however. I will make sure that I set aside two hours, preferably the same two hours, every day during the week and two hours in the mornings and two hours in the afternoons on weekends for study purposes.

8. I will notify everyone I know that typically I study between 7 and 9 P.M. and therefore not to call or disturb me until after 9 P.M.

9. If people do call or disturb me, I will tell them that I will get back in touch with them after 9 P.M.

When am I going to start and when am I going to finish working on my goal?

1. I will start working on increasing how long I study on Monday, January 15.

2. Since I know that I can't possibly get used to sitting still for two hours all at once, I will begin by increasing my study time to an hour and ten minutes. I will do this for 5 days, and then I will increase that to an hour and twenty minutes for 5 more days. I will thus systematically work myself up to two hours.

3. If I increase my limit every five days by taking on an additional ten minutes, it should take me 30 days to reach my goal.

Now do this with your goal. In the case of breaking the cigarette habit you may want to systematically decrease over a reasonable period of time the number of cigarettes you smoke on a daily basis. Decreasing them by one a day may work for you.

5. Establish a Stroke System to Help You Reach Your Goal

Whenever you're changing a specific behavior, it's a good idea to reward yourself with something you really enjoy doing. If, for instance, you really like to watch TV, listen to music, talk on the phone, eat ice cream, or read novels, make sure that you reward yourself with one of these activities immediately after you've finished putting in your designated amount of study time. Don't allow yourself to eat ice cream while you're studying; instead, get a bowl right after you've finished studying. You may want to schedule your study time so that you can be through when your favorite TV program is on the air, or you may want to call a friend every time you're through studying, thus rewarding yourself for time well spent.

If, however, you did not spend the time you had set aside to study well but instead sat behind your desk daydreaming, then you don't deserve to reward yourself. Instead you might make yourself work at something that you have to do but that is not a pleasurable reward —clean the kitchen floor, do the laundry, or pay your bills.

It's not a good idea to "punish" yourself by studying after your study time is up. It's not wise to use an activity that you want to learn to like as a punishment; when you pair undesirable study behavior with other undesirable behavior, you will eventually extinguish that behavior. You may eventually quit studying altogether.

Now go ahead and identify something that you thoroughly enjoy doing and begin doing it only after you have done what you're trying to learn to do.

6. Clarify How You and Others Will Know that Your Goal Has Been Reached

I will know that I have reached my goal when:
1. I can study for two hours at a time.
2. I feel that I have learned something during those two hours.
3. I know what's going on in my classes.
4. I feel prepared for my exams.
5. I feel like I can participate in class discussions if I want to.
6. My grades improve.
7. I feel that I've had sufficient time to digest what I have learned and to convert that into a data base I can use in day-to-day living and in my future career.
8. I feel better about my study habits and therefore about myself.

I will know that my teachers know that a change has taken place when:
1. They comment on my improved work.
2. They give me better grades.

I will know that my parents know that a change has taken place when:
1. They comment on my improved school work.
2. They comment on how well I can schedule my time.
3. They notice that I'm feeling better about myself.

7. *Write a Contract with Yourself*

Again, use the contract format provided in Chapter 10.

Exercise

As a group, practice using the action plan by applying it to the following hypothetical problems:

1. Breaking the cigarette habit.
2. Learning to enjoy spending time alone.
3. Suggest several more goals of your own.

Conclusion

Now that you know you can control who you are, where you want to go, and how you are going to get there, are you going to exercise that control?

Now that you know how to get in touch with and make use of your feelings, are you going to allow yourself to feel?

Now that you know how to analyze and build on your data base, are you going to continue to systematically sift and sort through new incoming data?

Now that you know how to integrate your "shoulds," your feelings, and factual data, are you going to approach life situations from that balanced state?

Now that you know that, if you need and want to, you can decide to change your general attitude toward yourself and others, are you going to do that?

Now that you know you can modify your behavior so that you can get greater satisfaction from how you behave with others, are you going to do that?

Now that you know you can be empathetic and genuine in how you give, take, and receive in any given life situation, are you going to exercise that option?

Now that you know you can choose to balance your time between work and play, are you going to do that?

Now that you know you have a method for analyzing your verbal and nonverbal exchanges with others, are you going to use it?

Now that you know that you can change what you want to change in yourself, are you going to opt to do that?

Index

199